'Therefore, you noble
Iraqi people, who
are equal to my father
and mother (in stature),
strike your enemy
strongly and accurately,
with the force of
the spirit of jihad
that you possess '

Saddam Hussein

The first Tomahawk cruise missile to be fired in the war is launched from the USS Bunker Hill at 5.15am local time on March 20

The Daily Telegraph
WAR
ON SADDAM

Introduction by
John Keegan
Narrative by
Ben Rooney
Special reports by
Michael Smith & Kim Fletcher

With despatches from
Martin Bentham, Patrick Bishop, David Blair,
Tim Butcher, Jack Fairweather,
Stewart Payne, Oliver Poole, Alex Spillius,
Julian Strauss, Neil Tweedie, Isambard Wilkinson

ROBINSON
London

CONTENTS

THE NARRATIVE

By Ben Rooney: including

DESPATCHES: THE WAR AS IT HAPPENED

16 reports from Daily Telegraph reporters in the field

Clouds on the horizon as
oil fires burn at the end
of the road to Baghdad

INTRODUCTION
JOHN KEEGAN ON THE MYSTERY OF SADDAM'S DOWNFALL

The Gulf war of 2003 closes, it may be hoped, a period of more than 20 years of military disturbance in the Gulf region. In 1980 Saddam Hussein, who had recently risen to power as head of the Ba'ath regime in Iraq, decided to open hostilities against the neighbouring state of Iran. The pretext was a dispute over the alignment of the frontier between the two countries but the occasion was a breakdown in normal relations between Iran and the United States, brought about by the fall of the Shah and the seizure of the American embassy in Teheran by the Islamic regime which had succeeded him. Saddam saw in the crisis an opportunity to annex the Iranian province of Khuzestan, inhabited in the majority by Arabs, kin to Iraqi Arabs across the border.

The Iran-Iraq war was bitter and prolonged, lasting from 1980 to 1988 and causing the deaths of half a million Iraqis and perhaps a million Iranians. It was ended eventually by a tacit Iraqi concession but not public acknowledgement of defeat. The costs, financial as well as human, nearly ruined Iraq and led directly to Saddam's next strategic venture, the annexation of Kuwait in August 1990. Iraq had been financed during the war with Iran by subventions from other Arab states, notably Saudi Arabia, which hoped that by supporting Saddam they could hold at bay, and perhaps even overcome, the forces of popular Islamicism that threatened their grip on power in their home countries. After the war was over they nevertheless demanded reimbursement for the payments made. Iraq was unable to meet its debts.

Saddam perceived a way out of his difficulty by seizing Kuwait, which was rich in oil and had long been claimed by his and previous Iraqi governments as part of the national territory. The claim, originating in ancient Ottoman imperial pretensions over the region,

had always been disputed by Great Britain, which had recognised and protected Kuwait as an independent emirate since before the Great War. Kuwait's independence had subsequently been underpinned by the United States. When, on August 2, Iraq invaded Kuwait and announced the state's incorporation into Iraq, official protests from Britain and America immediately followed. On their rejection, President George Bush began at once to organise both a diplomatic and a military coalition against Iraq. The UN Security Council condemned the Iraqi invasion and required a withdrawal. More than 60 states, eventually including numbers of Arab countries such as Egypt and Syria, aligned themselves with the United States, which at an early stage after the invasion began to lay military plans to reverse it, to prepare an intervention force and to organise command and control for a multinational expedition.

By early January an enormous concentration of air, ground and sea forces had been assembled, the bulk of it American, largely based in Saudi Arabia. Saddam remained intransigent nonetheless and on January 17, 1991, the coalition opened a devastating air campaign against his forces in Kuwait and on his headquarters in Iraq. It continued relentlessly even after the opening of the general offensive on February 24 and effectively destroyed the preferred positions of the Iraqi army and its command and control centres wherever located.

The ground offensive lasted only a hundred hours. Twelve divisions, including one British and one French light armoured division, had been deployed on an arc extending

In view of the complete failure of Saddam's military adventures against both Iran and Kuwait, it is astonishing that he should have been prepared to risk a third defeat only 12 years after his second humiliation

Cartoons from The Daily Telegraph by Garland

"FRANKLY MY DEAR, I DON'T GIVE A DAMN!"

"YOU WERE ONLY SUPPOSED TO BLOW THE BLOODY DOORS OFF"

"YOU TALKIN' TO ME?"

"INFAMY, INFAMY, THEY'VE ALL GOT IT IN FOR ME!"

POLL OF CINEMA'S GREATEST ONE-LINERS   (News Item)

around the Iraqi positions, outflanking them from the west. With continuous close air support, the divisions broke through the Iraqi defences, at almost no cost to themselves, rounded up the enemy mobile forces and drove the survivors back into Kuwait and southern Iraq. The Iraqi air force, which put up almost no resistance, had fled to Iran on January 28. Kuwait City was liberated on February 26 and a ceasefire requested that day. Ceasefire talks began on March 3.

In view of the complete and costly failure of Saddam's military adventures against both Iran and in Kuwait, it is astonishing that he should have been prepared to risk a third defeat only 12 years after his second humiliation. So, nevertheless, proved to be the case.

Saddam was undoubtedly possessed by powerful ambition, both personal and as a national leader. A man of humble origin, he had risen to power by the exercise of strong will and a readiness to use violence whenever opposed. He had taken great risks to ascend to the leadership of the Ba'ath Party and, once installed, had exacted a murderous revenge on his internal enemies. He seemed also able to represent reality to himself in ways that suited his personal vision of his own and his country's destiny. Because he had retained control of the national territory after the close of the Iran war, disastrous though it had been, he apparently persuaded himself that he had been victorious. Similarly, after the 1991 Gulf war, he insisted on representing the outcome as a success. The coalition had not exploited his military defeat to topple him from power. He had, by ruthless repression, crushed the widespread

Before the outbreak of war, Sir John Keegan, left, with Charles Moore, centre, editor of The Daily Telegraph, meets Donald Rumsfeld, the US Secretary of Defence, in Washington

internal revolts which followed, particularly in the northern Kurdish regions and in the Shi'ite south.

His survival apparently emboldened him to defy all subsequent efforts by the international community to bring him to heel. Those were motivated chiefly by his possession and use of chemical and biological weapons and his desire to acquire nuclear weapons. In 1981, the Israeli air force had destroyed his Osirak nuclear reactor, supplied by France, which would eventually have provided him with weapons-grade nuclear material.

He persisted in the acquisition of chemical weapons, which he used during the Iran war and against his Kurdish subjects. Beginning in the aftermath of the Gulf war of 1991 the United States and Britain, but without Security Council endorsement, had imposed restrictions on Saddam's military activity, defining "no-fly" zones both in the north and south, while the UN had instituted a programme of inspection on Iraqi territory to identify sites where illegal weapons were stored or manufactured and to destroy them.

It was Saddam's reluctance to co-operate in the inspection programme, leading to the withdrawal of the inspectors in December 1998, which led directly to the inception of the war in March 2003. After the outrage of the al-Qa'eda attack on the United States on September 11, 2001, the American government became determined to take active measures against hostile Islamic forces whenever identifiable.

The opening stage of the counter-offensive was the successful war against the Taliban in Afghanistan, where al-Qa'eda was based, in

"ACTION!"

2002. Washington then turned its attention to Iraq, which it believed both sponsored Islamic terrorism and was continuing to acquire weapons of mass destruction for purposes hostile to Western interests.

Working through the Security Council, it achieved the passage of a resolution, 1441, requiring Iraq to submit to renewed inspection of its territory or to expect serious consequences. Continued Iraqi frustration of the inspection scheme led to the dispatch of American and British expeditionary contingents to Kuwait and to the war that followed.

The 2003 Gulf war repeated the pattern of 1991, but in irrational and eventually bewildering form. Saddam, confronted by the overwhelming power of America's military machine, made a public face of behaving as if he opposed it with equivalent force. Threatened with attack, he made no concessions and offered no basis for compromise. He remained intransigent up to the moment when American and British forces crossed the Iraq-Kuwait border and began the methodical destruction of his defences.

The disparity in strength between the two sides was so extreme that comparisons with past conflicts are difficult to advance. During the 1980s Iraq had acquired, through gift or loan, huge quantities of up-to-date equipment for its army and air force, largely from the Soviet Union, though France was generous also. It was these modern weapons that had largely allowed it to survive the war with much more populous Iran in 1980-88. In the 1991 Gulf war it had nevertheless been at a severe material disadvantage and as a result of its defeat, had also lost large quantities of tanks, armoured vehicles and artillery pieces. These losses were not made good, largely because of

the fall of the Soviet Union, so that by 2003 Saddam's once-powerful forces were seriously outdated. His air force, of only a hundred or so aircraft, could not be risked in combat. The most modern of his tanks were 15 years old and were outranged and outgunned; the older models were museum pieces. To heighten the disadvantage under which Saddam's army fought, he appeared to have devised no logical plan of defence. Iraq is a difficult country to attack, since it possesses strong natural defences, broad expanses of desert on the west, mountains to the east and wide rivers in the centre, barring the way to the centres of population.

Attack is particularly difficult from the south, the coalition's point of entry, for the frontier with Kuwait and on the Gulf is very narrow and the distance to be covered to the capital is several hundred miles.

Logic suggested that, once invasion threatened, the southern sector should have been heavily mined, the port facilities sabotaged and, above all, the bridges over the Tigris and Euphrates prepared for demolition. None of these measures seem to have been taken. There was little troop strength in the south and little effort made to use natural obstacles to delay the invaders' advance. Resistance was organised at the most obvious points, such as road intersections, which could be easily outflanked.

Moreover, the organised forces available to Saddam were not employed or deployed in a rational way. In orthodox military planning, the best troops, the six divisions of the Republican Guard, would have been used to oppose the invading force, with the second line, the so-called regular army, committed to reinforce it where action was joined. The third line, consisting of the paramilitary Fedayeen and Ba'ath Party militia, would have operated only as a harassing force against the enemy's rear and flanks.

In practice, the deployment was exactly the other way about. The Republican Guard was kept out of the opening battle, far to the rear, in positions around Baghdad. Some divisions of the regular army appear to have opposed the invasion in the south but quickly melted away, the soldiers apparently divesting themselves of uniforms and weapons and taking refuge at home. Only the paramilitaries put up strong and consistent resistance, which they were unequipped to do. They fought because, individually, they were loyal to the Ba'athist system but also out of fear of revenge at the hands of the population.

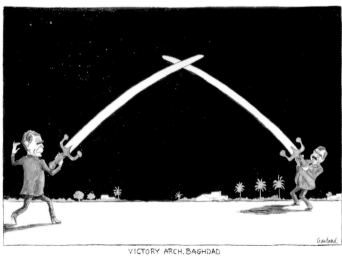

VICTORY ARCH, BAGHDAD

Once the coalition troops reached Baghdad, the Republican Guard entered the battle but, stricken by coalition airpower and completely outgunned in combat, were rapidly overcome.

In commenting on the war as it developed, I found myself constantly referring to its character as "mysterious". I find in retrospect no reason to choose another word. The pattern of the war was indeed mysterious. Why were Iraq's forces not deployed in a logical fashion? Why was so little effort made by the defenders to oppose the invaders in the south of the country, at a distance from strategic objectives? Why, given that the threat of an invasion had loomed for many months before it was launched, did the Iraqi high command not put obstacles and fixed defences in place? Why were targets of value, such as port facilities and the southern oilfields, not prepared for destruction? Why, above all, were the bridges over the two great rivers, the Euphrates and Tigris, the country's principal physical defences, either not prepared for demolition or, in so far as they were, not demolished on the approach of the coalition forces? Had the bridges been blown, the advance to Baghdad would have been much less rapid and much more difficult than was the case in practice.

The explanation of the failure to mount an adequate defence may lie in the palpable absence of any effort at national leadership by Saddam Hussein himself or his closest associates. The war was completely one-sided. While the leadership of the coalition was manifest and visible throughout, the Iraqi leadership was invisible.

That added to the war's mystery. Where was Saddam? Perhaps he was killed or disabled by air strike in the conflict's opening hours. Perhaps, however, he was not. There is no physical proof of his demise, nor any news of his fate in the aftermath.

Physically, the coalition achieved a great victory, at virtually no cost to itself and at little national cost to Iraq or its population. Its centres of population, the government quarter in Baghdad apart, were left undamaged. There were few casualties among the civilian population and Iraqi military casualties were not numerous. Nevertheless, the psychological cost to Iraq, to the Muslim Middle East and to the wider Muslim world, will undoubtedly prove very great.

Islam achieved its initial success as a self-proclaimed world religion in the seventh and eighth centuries by military conquest. It con-

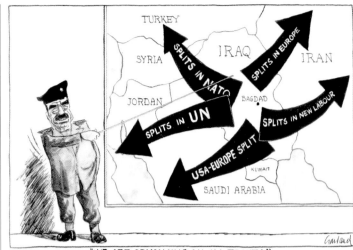

"WE ARE ADVANCING ON ALL FRONTS."

Physically, the coalition achieved a great victory, at virtually no cost to itself and at little national cost to Iraq or its population

solidated its achievement by the exercise of military power which, perpetuated by the Ottoman Caliphate, maintained Islam as the most important polity in the northern hemisphere until the beginning of the 18th century. Islam's decline in the three centuries that have followed embittered Muslims everywhere, but particularly those of its heartland in the Middle East. Muslims, convinced of the infallibility of their belief system, are merely outraged by demonstrations of the unbelievers' material superiority, particularly their military superiority. The Ba'ath Party, of which Saddam was leader in Iraq, was founded to achieve a Muslim renaissance; to his credit, Saddam created in Iraq, as Ba'athism requires, a secular society, respecting Islam but rejecting Muslim obscurantism.

The failure of the Ba'athist idea, which can only be emphasised by the fall of Saddam, will encourage militant Islamic fundamentalists, who have espoused the idea that the unbelievers' mastery of military techniques can be countered only by terror, to pursue novel and alternative methods of resistance to the unbelievers' power. Western civilisation, rooted in the idea that the improvement of the human lot lies in material advance and the enlargement of individual opportunity, is all-equipped to engage with a creed which deplores materialism and rejects the concept of individuality, particularly individual freedom. The defeat of Saddam has achieved a respite, an important respite, in the contest between the Western Way and its Muslim alternative. It has not, however, secured a decisive success. The very completeness of Western victory in Iraq ensures the continuation of the conflict.

WORDS OF A WARRIOR

An eve-of-battle address by Lt Col Tim Collins moved the nation. This is what he said

Lt Col Collins of the 1st Battn Royal Irish Regiment

'We go to liberate not to conquer. We will not fly our flags in their country We are entering Iraq to free a people and the only flag which will be flown in that ancient land is their own. Show respect for them. There are some who are alive at this moment who will not be alive shortly. Those who do not wish to go on that journey, we will not send. As for the others, I expect you to rock their world. Wipe them out if that is what they choose. But if you are ferocious in battle remember to be magnanimous in victory.

Iraq is steeped in history. It is the site of the Garden of Eden, of the Great Flood and the birthplace of Abraham. Tread lightly there. You will see things that no man could pay to see and you will have to go a long way to find a more decent, generous and upright people than the Iraqis. You will be embarrassed by their hospitality, even though they have nothing. Don't treat them as refugees, for they are in their own country. Their children will be poor: in years to come they will know that the light of liberation in their lives was brought by you.

If there are casualties of war, then remember that when they woke up and got dressed in the morning they did not plan to die this day. Allow them dignity in death. Bury them properly and mark their graves.

It is my foremost intention to bring every single one of you out alive but there may be people among us who will not see the end of this campaign. We will put them in their sleeping bags and send them back. There will be no time for sorrow. The enemy should be in no doubt that we are his nemesis and that we are bringing about his rightful destruction. There are many regional commanders who have stains on their souls and they are stoking the fires of hell for Saddam. He and his forces will be destroyed by this coalition for what they have done. As they die they will know their deeds have brought them to this place. Show them no pity. It is a big step to take another human life. It is not to be done lightly. I know of men who have taken life needlessly in other conflicts. I can assure you they live with the mark of Cain upon them.

If someone surrenders to you then remember they have that right in international law and ensure that one day they go home to their family. The ones who wish to fight, well, we aim to please. If you harm the regiment or its history by over-enthusiasm in killing or in cowardice, know it is your family who will suffer. You will be shunned unless your conduct is of the highest, for your deeds will follow you down through history. We will bring shame on neither our uniform nor our nation.

It is not a question of if, it's a question of when. We know he has already devolved the decision to lower commanders, and that means he has already taken the decision himself. If we survive the first strike we will survive the attack. As for ourselves, let's bring everyone home and leave Iraq a better place for us having been there. Our business now is north.

TURKEY

SYRIA

CYPRUS

ISRAEL

JORDAN

IRAQ
Baghdad

IRAN

KUWAIT

EGYPT

SAUDI ARABIA

QATAR

200 miles

Tikrit 60 miles

River Tigris

2

1

BAGHDAD

River Euphrates

Karbala

Hilla

Najaf

Key

Strategic bridge

(8) Highway

1 Major road

Allied advance

March 21

March 23

March 29

April 8

SAUDI ARABIA

THE SECRET WAR
MICHAEL SMITH ON THE HIGH-TECH HUNT FOR INTELLIGENCE

In the 1991 Gulf war it took six hours to get intelligence to front-line commanders. In 2003, thanks to the internet, it was a matter of minutes

The secret war, the hunt for intelligence, was absolutely vital to the war in Iraq. The Pentagon's decision to keep the number of ground forces to a minimum, the so-called "battle lite" option, meant that the allies depended heavily on intelligence being delivered in what the military calls "real time". During the 1991 Gulf war, the allies used large numbers of ground troops, relying on overwhelming force to ensure they won. During the 2003 war, the proponents of battle lite, chief among them Donald Rumsfeld, the US Defence Secretary, argued that the allies' overwhelming air power allowed them to use far fewer forces. But it relied on getting the intelligence to commanders quickly, to cut the length of the so-called kill chain, the time between the intelligence being acquired and the target being attacked. Not as easy as might be believed.

America and Britain enjoy an unrivalled ability to collect intelligence on their enemies, and indeed their friends, and have done so since the Second World War, when the Anglo-American intelligence relationship began. Its beginnings were encouraged by the successes of the British codebreakers at Bletchley Park in breaking the German Enigma ciphers. Despite that success and its undoubted effect on the war, commanders in the field rarely received the intelligence produced by the codebreakers in anything like real time.

The Bletchley Park reports on what was going on in North Africa reached commanders in the field at best three hours later, but the average was around six hours. Perhaps more surprisingly, by the 1991 Gulf war, the kill chain or sensor-to-shooter time was pretty

Eight hours before the war began special forces flew into Iraq to destroy Iraqi command posts, in particular those used to launch chemical and biological weapons

The heavy dependence of the relatively light allied forces on accurate, real-time intelligence was highlighted by two intelligence failures

much the same as it had been in 1942. It was the only major failure of the 1991 Gulf war and the allies realised things had to change. The answer came in the form of the internet and the expanded use of satellite and computer technology, right down to the level of small units on the ground. These were the beginnings of what the military calls network centric-warfare. For the first time, front-line commanders were able to receive intelligence reports in real time, sent via the internet to small, but robust, portable computers on the front line.

The allies' intelligence can be separated into three types. The first was human intelligence, known in the jargon of the spy as HUMINT. This came from CIA and MI6 agents inside Iraq and from allied special forces such as the SAS and the US Delta Force on the ground inside Iraq. The second element of the intelligence package was imagery intelligence, IMINT – photographic, infra-red or radar-generated pictures collected by allied aircraft overflying Iraq and US satellites. Over the previous 12 years, allied aircraft and satellites had photographed every inch of Iraq, mapping out the positions of every government and military building. The third element was signals intelligence, SIGINT – the interception of electronic emissions from radio, telephone and radar, perhaps the most important of the allies' intelligence capabilities. Here again the allies had spent more than a decade recording every frequency and channel used by the Iraqi armed forces.

Human intelligence is normally the most difficult to track. Agents must be protected at all costs, particularly in such a brutal regime as Iraq. But the overt evidence of human intelligence was far greater in this war than ever before. It was already clear from the evidence released in the British dossier on Iraqi weapons of mass destruction that either MI6 or the CIA had a number of human intelligence sources inside the Iraqi regime. In the months leading up to the invasion, these would be augmented by teams of allied special forces. British, American and Australian forces operate together in Joint Special Operations Task Forces (JSOTF). Two such forces were formed for Iraq, one to cover the northern area controlled by the Kurds, and one for the rest of Iraq. The special forces operating in the north worked with the Kurdish guerrillas, the peshmerga. These operations were based on what might be described as the Afghanistan model, with allied special forces training and co-ordinating the guerrillas, an important role given that in the absence of a substantial northern front they would form the main fighting force to take the northern cities of Kirkuk and Mosul.

The allied special forces in southern and western Iraq operated from forward bases in Kuwait and, despite their public refusal to allow allied forces to mount attacks on Iraq from their territory, in Saudi Arabia and Jordan. Their pre-war roles included reconnaissance of the Iraqi command and control system and Iraqi military positions to check that potential targets spotted using satellite intelligence were not dummy targets, which had been widely used in the 1991 war.

Eight hours before the war began, allied special forces flew into southern and western Iraq to destroy Iraqi command posts, in particular those that were to be used to launch chemical and biological weapons. They also destroyed key junctions in the fibre-optic communications links to disrupt the Iraqi command-and-control system, forcing Iraqi military communications up on to the airwaves, where they could be monitored by the allies. The Special Boat Service, which specialised in protecting the North Sea oilfields from terrorist attack, secured oil wells to pre-

US soldiers, below, work through the night at the allied forward command post at Doha, Qatar. In a war in which knowing your enemy's movements is vital, the laptop can be as deadly as a gun

vent the Iraqis from setting them on fire. It also carried out reconnaissance for the Royal Marine amphibious assault on the Faw peninsula. A key role for the SAS was to be a reprise of their main operations during the 1991 Gulf war, ensuring that the Iraqis could not use their remaining Scud missiles to attack Israel in order to bring it into the war. This would have complicated allied strategy and caused problems for those Arab countries that were allowing the allies to base troops or command posts on their territory. The SAS was also given the task of searching for weapons of mass destruction.

The special forces were not the only allied asset to enter Iraq before the war began. Predator and Global Hawk unmanned aerial vehicles, piloted by remote control, began flying over the planned allied routes carrying out reconnaissance and logging targets, relaying real-time video footage of what was going on in Iraq directly to allied commanders.

High-flying aerial reconnaissance aircraft such as the American U2 and the RAF's PR9 were also operating, as was the American Joint Surveillance Target Attack Radar System, a modified Boeing 707 airliner, which flew along the border to build up a complete pic-

ture of everything on the ground for more than 150 miles into enemy territory. Much further up in the sky the US Keyhole and Lacrosse satellite systems were collecting a mass of photographic, infra-red and radar imagery. All of this was sent back by satellite to Britain's Joint Air Reconnaissance Intelligence Centre at Brampton, just outside Huntingdon, for interpretation.

But it was human intelligence that played the key role in the aerial strikes that began the war. A "very good" CIA source reported that Saddam Hussein and his two sons, Uday and Qusay, would be sleeping in a building close to Baghdad University on the night of March 19. The Dora Farm complex belonged to Saddam's youngest daughter Hala and her husband, who was Saddam's private secretary. It was this information, passed on to President Bush by George Tenet, the director of the CIA, which led to the "decapitation attempt" that opened the war.

Intelligence, almost certainly from signals intelligence, suggested that someone important in the complex that night had needed a blood transfusion and may even have died. The encrypted communications system used by Saddam's lieutenants to communicate with the rest of the Iraqi leadership remained silent following the attack, encouraging the belief that the Iraqi dictator might have been killed.

British signals intelligence operations are controlled by the Government Communications Headquarters (GCHQ), which is based at Cheltenham and shares coverage of the world with its US counterpart, the National Security Agency.

Operations against Arabic-speaking countries in the Middle East are led by GCHQ, through a Joint Services Signal Unit at Ayios Nikolaos in Cyprus, formerly known as 9 Signal Regiment. Since the 1991 Gulf war, this unit has also manned forward intercept sites in Jordan and Kuwait.

Two US spy satellites, one of which is permanently above the Indian Ocean, intercept other Iraqi communications, including radio telephone signals. The "take" from these satellite intercepts is downloaded at Morwenstow, in Cornwall, and sent to another Joint Services Signal Unit at Digby, in Lincolnshire, for transcription.

During the war, these operations were reinforced by around a dozen signals intelligence reconnaissance aircraft known in the jargon as "aerial platforms", on which signals operators intercepted a range of electronic signals from mobile telephones to air defence

A CIA tip-off that Saddam was staying, with his sons, Uday, top, and Qusay, at a farm complex belonging to his daughter was the trigger that started the war

radars. They included at least one R1 Nimrod from RAF Waddington, in Lincolnshire.

The ground war began within hours of the aerial strike on the Dora Farm complex, with allied special forces providing intelligence on the ground. While the SBS, working with their American counterparts, the Seals, were leading the allied advance into southern Iraq, SAS troops accompanied by US special forces and supported by Royal Marines from 45 Commando flew in by helicopter from Jordan. They opened up a second front in the west and captured the western Iraqi airfields at H2 and H3, named after the oil pumping stations along the old Haifa-Baghdad pipeline.

The heavy dependence of the relatively light allied force on accurate real-time intelligence was highlighted by two intelligence failures. Signals intelligence was probably behind reports on March 26, a week into the war, of large numbers of Republican Guard tanks heading south from Baghdad to meet the advancing US marines. The allied advance had been halted by heavy sandstorms and the Republican Guards' T72s would have represented a serious threat to the lightly armoured marines.

The sandstorms had blinded the Global Hawks and Predators, making intercepted Iraqi communications the most easily available source of intelligence. But several hours later, after radar imagery that could see through the sandstorms was evaluated, the Pentagon ruled out an Iraqi counter-attack, saying that the Republican Guard redeployments were merely "defensive repositioning". The false reports were almost certainly based on a misreading of the significance of the large amounts of communications required to reposition the Republican Guard troops during the sandstorms.

That was a relatively minor mistake compared with the failure of the allied intelligence services to give sufficient credibility to the ability of the Saddam Fedayeen to attack the allies and, particularly, the lightly armoured US marines. A series of attacks on US marines passing through a major choke point at Nasiriyah – where the allies' eastern route towards Baghdad crossed two bridges across the Euphrates – caused problems for the American troops that were out of all proportion to the respective strengths of the two opposing forces.

The solution was again intelligence-based and provided by the allied special forces. Intelligence showed that the Fedayeen were trained in Baghdad and then sent to a forward operating base in a race course in Diwaniyah, a town 100 miles south of the Iraqi capital, from where their operations against the allied forces were co-ordinated.

Groups of Fedayeen were being sent from Diwaniyah to a command post in the railway station in Nasiriyah. Special forces teams used laser designators to call in aerial attacks on all three bases, causing major disruption to the Fedayeen operations, which never recovered.

The British proceeded far more cautiously in their attempts to take Basra, Iraq's second city, using a classic British "hearts and minds" policy. The phrase, much misused during the war, refers to tactics originally worked out to deal with communist guerrillas in Malaya in the early 1950s.

Much was made of the way in which the British cordon around the city leaked refugees. But a hearts and minds operation is intelligence-led. Allowing people to come in and out provided a steady flow of ready, and grateful, informants who could reveal what was going on and where Saddam Hussein's men were hiding.

The British troops took the city piece by piece. Having gathered every shred of intelligence they could on who was where in the first target sector, they moved in, conducting house-to-house searches in order to turn it "white", to cleanse it of Saddam's henchmen. Once the people of that first sector were liberated they in turn provided more intelligence on the neighbouring sectors, allowing the British troops to move on to occupy these.

The key piece of intelligence came on Friday March 28 when the British received information from inside the city that 200 Saddam loyalists were holding a meeting in the city's Ba'ath Party headquarters. Two US F15E Strike Eagle ground attack aircraft bombed the building. Resistance inside Basra collapsed not long after the attack, allowing the British to go in and take the entire city.

American troops had planned to begin the attack on Baghdad itself on Sunday March 30 but when the allies intercepted radio communications ordering the Republican Guard divisions based south of the capital to pull back they decided to wait. As the Republican Guards moved out of their dug-in positions they came under heavy bombardment from a mass of allied aircraft. The concerted attack effectively took all but a few remnants of the Republican Guard out of the battle for Baghdad. Signals intelligence played a key role in telling coalition commanders about the sorry state of Iraqi command and control. By early April, intercepted high-level communications were revealing that Saddam's brutal younger son Qusay was still alive and controlling the Iraqi resistance. But so terrified were senior Iraqi officers of what he might do that they repeatedly spoke of having defeated the American troops in battle and claimed to have inflicted high levels of casualties on coalition forces.

On April 8, an intercepted message revealed that more than two dozen other members of the Iraqi leadership, possibly including Saddam, if he was still alive, and at least one of his sons, were meeting at a house next to the al-Saa restaurant in the Mansur district of north-west Baghdad that afternoon. The message confirmed reports from two human intelligence agents on the ground.

"Intelligence indicated that there would definitely be senior leadership, including Saddam Hussein, at a meeting in that structure," one source said. "If Saddam did not slip out, then he is dead."

The precise co-ordinates of the house were reported to Central Command's forward command post at Qatar and relayed on to the Combined Air Operations Centre at Prince Sultan Air Base in Saudi Arabia with orders to destroy the target within half an hour of the information's being intercepted.

A B1 Lancer bomber on its way to attack a number of targets inside Iraq was diverted to bomb the house using four satellite-guided bunker-buster bombs. The first two were designed to penetrate the structure of the building and the second two were set with a time delay to ensure that the complete complex was brought down.

The time between the message indicating that Saddam would be in the building to the time the first bomb dropped – the so-called sensor-to-shooter time – was only 45 minutes. But it seems that it was still too long and that if Saddam was in the restaurant he had indeed slipped out in time.

"We think we just missed him," one British intelligence official said. "You can never predict it. You get the information at 4pm and by 4.45 when you hit it, he's gone."

But whether or not Saddam was still alive, the cutting of the kill chain from the six hours of the Second World War to a matter of minutes was a defining moment in the use of intelligence on the battlefield.

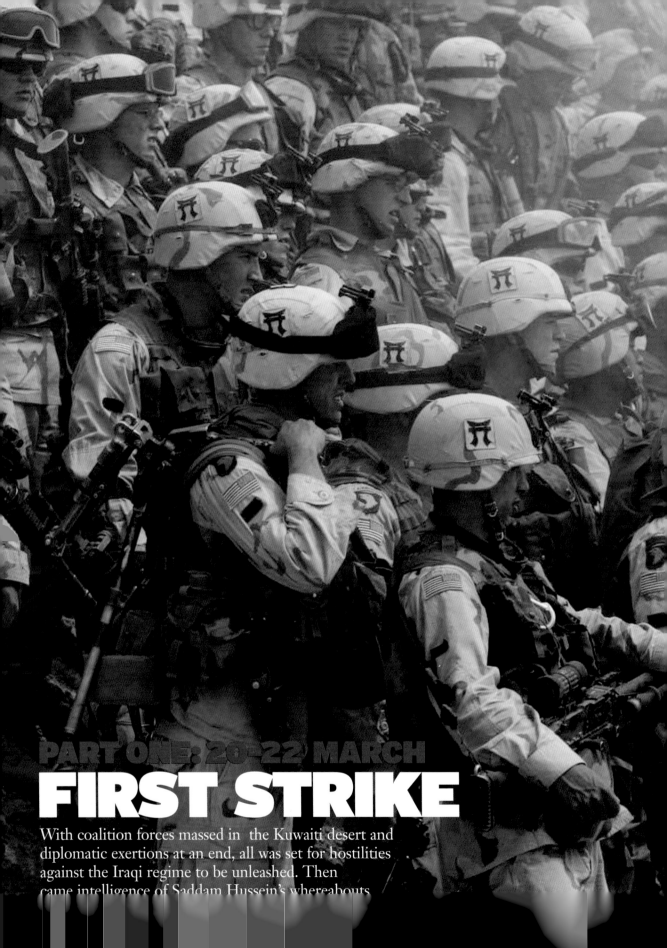

FIRST STRIKE

With coalition forces massed in the Kuwaiti desert and
diplomatic exertions at an end, all was set for hostilities
against the Iraqi regime to be unleashed. Then
came intelligence of Saddam Hussein's whereabouts

eorge Tenet was at his desk in the New Headquarters Building of the CIA, at Langley, Virginia, when the call came through. It was shortly before 3pm (11pm Baghdad time), on Wednesday, March 19. They had a fix on Saddam. They knew exactly where he was sleeping that night. Right down to the very building – in a bunker hidden beneath a residential compound known as Dora Farm, near Baghdad University, in the south east of the Iraqi capital.

Cutting across the Washington traffic, the 18th director of the Central Intelligence Agency sped towards the Pentagon. Brushing past the two US marines on sentry duty in the

DAY 1 20.03.03
Previous page: US soldiers from the 3rd Brigade of the 101st Airborne Division assemble ready to move to forward positions in the Kuwaiti desert only hours before the opening of hostilities

Eisenhower Corridor outside the office of Donald Rumsfeld, the Defence Secretary, he burst in. Already there was his hawkish deputy, Paul Wolfowitz.

Here was a chance to end the war before it had even begun. If Saddam and his regime leaders could be killed in a "decapitating strike", hundreds and maybe thousands of lives could be spared.

The three men picked up the Chairman of the Joint Chiefs of Staff, Air Force General Richard Myers, en route, and raced across the Potomac River to the White House for a hastily convened meeting with President George W Bush, his National Security Adviser, Condoleezza Rice, and Andrew Card,

the White House chief of staff. Mr Tenet did not need to explain to the 57-year-old President the importance of the news. There was, however, a problem. Saddam was deep inside one of his many bunkers. A cruise missile would barely chip the yards-thick concrete walls of the German-designed shelter. If they were to stand a chance of killing him, they had to use the 2000lb, GBU31 "Bunker Buster" – and more than one.

It was a huge risk. To launch an attack now would mean sending in aircraft against Baghdad's still intact air defences on a clear moonlit night. But it was too good an opportunity to pass. President Bush called Gen Tommy Franks, the commander of US forces

in the Gulf at his headquarters in Doha, Qatar. At 6.30pm Washington time, President Bush gave the order.

Within the hour, hundreds of miles away at the Al Udeid base in Qatar, a pair of F117A Nighthawk stealth fighters from the 49th Fighter Wing, usually based at Holloman Air Force Base, New Mexico, taxied out on to the 15,000ft runway – the longest runway in the Gulf. Each plane carried a pair of the 2,000lb satellite-guided penetrator bombs. The aircraft disappeared into the night, to make the 700-mile journey north to Iraq on their top-secret mission.

Meanwhile, Gen Franks ordered a cruise missile attack against the bunker and other key

British troops gather in the Kuwaiti sand to receive a pep talk and briefing from Lt-Gen Jeff Conway, Commanding General of the I Marine Expeditionary Force

command and control buildings in the Iraqi capital. To eight American warships in the Gulf, the co-ordinates of Saddam's bunker and other targets were transmitted in an encrypted top-secret flash message. Some 40 cruise missiles were programmed for launch from the armada on station in the Persian Gulf, the Red Sea and the Mediterranean.

On board the USS Bunker Hill, a 10,000-ton Ticonderoga-class guided missile cruiser escorting the aircraft carrier USS Constellation, Captain Faris Farwell made an announcement over the ship's intercom.

"We are in receipt of Tomahawk tasking," he told the ship's crew of 24 officers and 340 men. "Your Commander-in-Chief said, 'We

will not falter, we will not tire, we will not fail'. Following 9/11, gentlemen and ladies, you have not faltered, or tired, and we will not fail." He concluded: "God bless the USS Bunker Hill. God bless America."

The Bunker Hill, sailing some 25 miles off the Iraqi coastline, went to battle stations. At the same time the F117A Nighthawk stealth fighters slipped into Iraqi airspace. On board the $122million aircraft the pilots scanned their electronic protection suites, searching for the tell-tale radar signature that an Iraqi surface-to-air missile battery had detected them. There was nothing. The planes pushed on towards the capital.

At 5.15am, Baghdad time, aboard the

Bunker Hill, Capt Farwell gave the order, "Batteries release". The ship slammed into the water as the first of the 18ft Tomahawk cruise missiles – weighing 2,650lb and costing about $600,000 – shot out of a tube and rose up over the slate gray Persian Gulf in a low arc, heading north. More missiles followed quickly. Crew members on deck cheered.

At 5.34am, the F117A Nighthawks dropped their deadly cargo. With pinpoint accuracy, the four bombs slammed into their target, penetrating deep into the concrete bunker before detonating with a deafening blast. A crushing shockwave ripped through the structure throwing up a massive plume of smoke and dust high into the pre-dawn sky.

Minutes later, the Tomahawks found their targets. Their 1,000lb warheads slammed into concrete and exploded. More missiles and bombs followed. Images of the explosions – which continued for about 10 minutes – were carried instantaneously via satellite around the world. Months of diplomatic wrangling had crossed into war – but had they got Saddam?

Although there was no one point in time at which the Bush administration had decided to focus its military might on the rogue regime, it was the horrific events of September 11, 2001, that sealed Saddam's fate.

For Vice-President Dick Cheney, the Defence Secretary during the 1991 Gulf war, the terrible destruction of the twin 110-storey towers of the World Trade Centre in lower Manhattan, and the attack on the very heart of the US military machine at the Pentagon in Washington, changed America's relationship with the rest of the world for ever.

Mr Cheney feared the leadership of the Clinton era had left America's enemies believing the superpower to be a 20-stone ▶24

weakling, unwilling or unable to use its crushing power. The debacle in Somalia had been the nadir of Pentagon power.

In Donald Rumsfeld, Mr Cheney had a spiritual ally. Rumsfeld, on his second tour as Defence Secretary (he had the unique distinction of being both the oldest, at 70, under President George W Bush, and the youngest, at 43, under President Ford), was determined to transform the US military into a high-tech, strategically nimble force that, most importantly, could be used quickly and effectively in the pursuit of US foreign policy.

Cheney and Rumsfeld became increasingly convinced that Iraq, armed with weapons of mass destruction, was the main threat to the safety of the United States. It was not a question of "if", but "when" Saddam would use them.

The Washington hawks believed it was conceivable, even probable, that he would use terrorists as a proxy force. For Baghdad, terrorists were ideal operatives – they had no "return address".

Saddam had to be stopped.

Across the Atlantic in Britain, Tony Blair found himself inexorably drawn to the same conclusion. As an avid consumer of the intelligence reports produced by MI6, even before September 11, the Prime Minister was deeply troubled by the proliferation of weapons of mass destruction. And many times he had shown himself willing to back diplomatic rhetoric with military muscle.

After September 11, Mr Blair was one of the first world leaders to give warning of the dangers of the marriage between terrorists and a state sponsor armed with weapons of mass destruction. He raised the pressure on Iraq, pressing for the unconditional re-introduction of weapons inspectors. He even recalled Parliament just after the anniversary of the September 11 attack.

Between the two allies, a twin-track approach was formed. Firstly, the military began to build up its forces in the Gulf. Five of America's mighty carriers, the USS Constellation, Kitty Hawk, Theodore Roosevelt, Abraham Lincoln and Harry S Truman, sailed from their usual stations patrolling the oceans of the world. Aircraft were sent from bases across America to the newly-built runways of the Persian Gulf, and soldiers and marines in their thousands began to flood into Kuwait. The 3rd US Infantry Division, "The Rock of the Marne", were ordered from their bases in Fort Stewart, Georgia. A brigade of parachutists from the

Previous page: Soldiers from the 3rd Brigade of the US 101st Airborne Division relax in foxholes by their convoy as they await their orders to advance into Iraq

DESPATCH
22.03.03 FROM ISAMBARD WILKINSON ON BOARD THE USS BUNKER HILL

THE STARTER BUTTON FOR WAR

The man who pressed the button to send the first Tomahawk cruise missiles of the war roaring towards Iraq was not in a reflective mood. "I am not paid to philosophise," said Petty Officer Clayton Bartels, 23.

The order for battle stations was received at 2.30am local time on the Bunker Hill, a Ticonderoga-class cruiser armed with 122 Tomahawk missiles and circling 25 miles off the Iraqi coast.

"This is for real," one sailor muttered as the crew stumbled out of their bunks.

The message to attack was passed to the ship from National Command Authority, via the US Navy's Fifth Fleet headquarters in Bahrain.

Just over an hour after the first call to arms, the 567ft cruiser became one of the first two vessels in the coalition fleet to be ordered into action. Behind a heavy metal hatch marked "Authorised Personnel Only", sailors' faces were reflected in the orange glow of more than 20 radar monitors. Bartels sat, with two fellow petty officers, at three computer consoles behind a black plastic curtain. At 5.15am the Firing Integrating System indicated that it was ready to launch 13 missiles on a touch screen with a Windows-style layout. Captain Faris Farwell reached to his left and turned a key. A green light came on and he gave the final order to fire with the innocuous words "Batteries release".

Petty Officer Bartels pressed the "execute" button in the bottom right of his screen. The entire ship was rammed hard down into the water by a succession of dull thuds as the missiles' grey hatches flipped open and the weapons blasted upwards. In a cloud of white smoke the 20ft white tubes were momentarily suspended in mid-air before their main engines ignited, lighting up the morning sky magnesium-bright. Arcing to one side, the missiles streaked across the sky. The crew cheered. Within minutes they were raining fire on their targets.

82nd Airborne Division, "The All Americans", boarded planes at Fort Bragg, North Carolina. The helicopters and men of the 101st Airborne (Air Assault) Division, "The Screaming Eagles", based at Fort Campbell, Kentucky, were dispatched as well.

Britain, too, prepared for its largest wartime deployment for a decade. Planning staff at Britain's Permanent Joint Headquarters at Northwood, in Middlesex, worked 24 hours a day to identify the brigades of soldiers to attack Iraq, the ships that would form Britain's largest flotilla since the Falklands war and the squadrons of aircraft for a strike force that comprised a quarter of the RAF's airpower. All the military needed was the order to go from the politicians.

Meanwhile, diplomats continued the grinding process of winning support. The diplomatic high watermark came on November 8, 2002, when the Security Council unanimously passed resolution 1441, designed to force Iraq to give up all weapons of mass destruction and threatening "serious consequences" if it did not comply.

Iraq accepted the terms of the resolution. But any hope that the crisis was over proved short-lived. On December 7, Baghdad handed the UN a 12,000-page document, claiming that it was a complete declaration of its entire chemical, biological, nuclear and missile programmes.

It wasn't. There were glaring inconsistencies between the report and the previous declarations the regime had made. Gallons of anthrax growth medium were unaccounted for, as were 8,000 tons of the chemical weapon, VX. The Americans declared Iraq to be in "material breach" of resolution 1441. Mr Blair was equally dismissive, accusing Baghdad of lying about its weapons capability. Officials said Blair began to realise then that Saddam was not serious about disarmament.

The military clock ticked ever louder. On January 7, Geoff Hoon, the Defence Secretary stood at the Despatch Box in front of a crowded House of Commons to announce the deployment of a large British force to the Gulf. Some 45,000 men, the soldiers of 7 Armoured Brigade, 16 Air Assault Brigade and 3 Commando Brigade would spearhead Britain's land force. Together with 100 fixed-wing aircraft and nearly 20 Royal Navy vessels, they would be dispatched under the code-name Operation Telic. Meanwhile, the telephone lines at 10 Downing Street were buzzing as Mr Blair worked flat out to secure a second UN resolution, explicitly autho- ▶28

Next page: Smoke billows over the Baghdad skyline as the presidential palace compound is targeted during a second night of intense allied air raids on the capital

DESPATCH
22.03.03 FROM STEWART PAYNE AT THE ALI AL SALEM AIRBASE, IN KUWAIT

TORNADOS LEAD BLITZ ON BAGHDAD

The RAF Tornado air crews who paved the way for the aerial bombardment of Baghdad returned safely to base last night and spoke of the awesome sight of the city erupting in flames.

"Baghdad was ablaze. There were explosions going off every few seconds," said Wing Cdr Derek Watson, who led his IX(B) Squadron. "We had anti-aircraft fire to one side and multiple rocket launchers were used against us. We could see the missiles but they were never a threat."

His Tornado GR4 precision bombers fired their air-launched, anti-radiation missiles (Alarm) to take out Baghdad's integrated air defence systems, opening the way for bombers to target Saddam and his high command. "We got our missiles off on time. We did the job," he said.

Baghdad was already under a huge missile attack when the Tornados arrived. Once the RAF fast jets had done their work, much more was to follow. "We had to fly through a wall of coalition aircraft waiting to go in behind us. We found our way through. It was in some ways the most dangerous part. There was so much up there," said Wing Cdr Watson, 39. "Once we were over Iraq it thinned out and we had the place to ourselves. When we approached Baghdad it was already a red glow on the horizon.

"The missiles were doing their work. But the Iraqis were still firing back. It is not over yet. The job is not finished."

All of IX(B) Squadron returned safely, as did the Tornados of 617 Squadron (The Dambusters) flying a separate mission. Wing Cdr Watson and his formation were in the air for two and a half hours. As his aircraft taxied to a halt he gave the thumbs up to his ground crew and turned to shake the hand of his navigator, Squadron Leader James Linter. "They talked about the attack on Baghdad being shocking and awesome, and that is what it was," said Sq Ldr Linter. "I would not have wanted to be on the receiving end."

▶ rising the use of military force against Iraq. Blair seemed convinced he could persuade the Security Council that, having passed a resolution calling for the disarmament of Iraq, they must see it through to its logical conclusion. He left himself an escape clause, however, warning that he would act without UN authority if there were an "unreasonable veto".

His hopes for UN blessing were dashed when President Jacques Chirac of France declared in early March that he would oppose *any* resolution authorising the use of force. At last Britain and America had the diplomatic excuse to go it alone.

Over the weekend of March 15/16, in a summit meeting at the Azores, Mr Blair, Mr Bush and the Spanish Prime Minister, Jose Maria Aznar, met to finalise diplomatic and military plans. It was clear to the three that Chirac's intransigence had dashed any hope of UN backing. Britain, America and Australia, which had recently committed its forces to any military action, would stand together.

Bush gave a final ultimatum. Saddam and his sons had 48 hours either to leave or to face the consequences. The sands of time for his regime would run out at 0100 GMT on Thursday March 20.

It fell to Sir Jeremy Greenstock, the urbane former Assistant Master at Eton and now Britain's ambassador to the United Nations, to bring down the final curtain on the diplomactic effort and clear the world's stage for war. On the Monday, March 17, he stood before the world's press to announce that the joint sponsors of the second resolution were withdrawing it. There would be no resolution. There would be no UN mandate.

In the face of huge political opposition, including splits in his own Cabinet, Mr Blair that day persuaded a fraught House of Commons to back military force. Robin Cook, a long-time opponent of military action resigned as Leader of the House. Claire Short, the International Development Secretary, vacillated, but eventually announced she would stay, leaving her political credibility in tatters. War was now inevitable.

Out in the sands of Kuwait, months of waiting were coming to an end. On Tuesday March 18, a force of hundreds of thousands of soldiers, sailors, airmen and marines, received their final orders. Months of planning were about to reach their final, and terrible, conclusion. Meanwhile, in Baghdad life continued in a surreal visage of normality. Shops remained

Top: A pin-up decorates the side of an armoured vehicle as a dust-covered marine awaits orders to advance

Above: Iraqi prisoners are taken after a gun battle with US marines of the India Company outside Az Bayer

open, cars moved about on the streets. There were sandbags on view, but no large movement of soldiers, no obvious signs of a capital that was about to have a maelstrom of violence unleashed upon it. In a final gesture of defiance, the Iraqi parliament rejected the American ultimatum.

Back in Washington on the evening of Wednesday March 19, the television networks received a call from the White House. President Bush would be making a live statement that evening.

Just before the cameras rolled, Mr Bush raised his left hand in a fist, shouting, "I feel good".

He settled at his desk in the Oval Office, a present to the American people from Queen Victoria and made from timbers of the warship Resolute. At 10.15pm, Washington time, he began his speech. "My fellow citizens, at this hour, American and coalition forces are in the early stages of military operations to disarm Iraq, to free its people and to defend the world from grave danger." The world knew the coalition was at war.

But the question now plaguing the leaders in Washington – had they got Saddam? – was

not to receive the answer they were hoping for. Three hours after the first strike, Iraqi television carried images of what it said was President Saddam Hussein. If it was him, then he was clearly shaken. Wearing large spectacles, and reading in a halting delivery, he vowed that Iraq would be victorious. It appeared the strike had failed.

The war went ahead.

The "decapitation" attack took the men out in the field by surprise. On a strict need-to-know basis, it had been judged that the soldiers on the ground did not need to know. Indeed, President Bush told Tony Blair himself only a few hours before the attack began. The first the ground forces knew that the war had started was when they heard news of it on the radio.

The next indication was when the radar screen of a Patriot missile operator lit up with an incoming track. From deep in the Faw peninsula the Iraqis launched at least four missiles: two believed to be Scud Bs, which Saddam had denied having. The other two were Silkworm-type anti-ship missiles fired at ground forces. An American Patriot missile battery shot one missile down. The others

A US marine keeps his rifle at the ready as Iraqi soldiers surrender outside the southern city of Safwan

detonated in the deserts of northern Kuwait.

In the first wave of the ground attack to be launched at 10pm local time on Thursday, March 20, were the men of 3 Commando Brigade under the command of Brig Jim Dutton. Their objective: to seize the oil facilities in the south. Ever since President Bush had given Saddam the ultimatum to quit Iraq, the men of 3 Commando Brigade had been on four hours' notice to move in case Saddam Hussein decided to order the flooding of the Gulf with crude oil.

Their orders on the first night were to grab the Faw peninsula. Faw had been identified as a strategic target. Its pumping station and two pipeheads – the main outlets for Iraqi oil – were vital, as Saddam could have caused chaos by blowing them up. No one knew what to expect. Many politicians had been talking up the parlous state of the Iraqi army, saying that it would surrender en masse and that the Allies' biggest problem would be dealing with the prisoners of war. Others, however, were not so sure.

As well as the men of 40 and 42 Commando, Brig Dutton had a US Marine Corps unit under him, the 15th Marine ▶34

DAY 2 21.03.03 A British soldier orders his men over the top of a berm into Iraq from their holding position in Kuwait

Iraqi civilians scream for help after being caught in crossfire as US marines advanced on the southern port of Umm Qasr

An Iraqi officer is given water from a marine's canteen. He was one of 200 who surrendered to US marines only an hour after they crossed into Iraq

DESPATCH

19.03.03 FROM PATRICK BISHOP ON THE KUWAIT/IRAQ BORDER

BIRDSONG IS THE PRELUDE TO BATTLE

The weight of the events that are about to unfold seemed all the more awesome at noon yesterday as the racket of the build-up in the border area mysteriously died away and the loudest noise in the stilled desert air was the sound of birdsong.

It was not so earlier. During the night, the silence was shattered several times by F16 fighters swooping low across the front lines in a manoeuvre that seemed designed to terrify the Iraqi troops lined up to the north. At breakfast time a long convoy of eight-wheeled armoured vehicles rolled up towards an American camp close to the front line. The helmets of the US marines clustered on top, the scarves wrapped around their faces and the wraparound sunglasses blotting out their features gave them a timeless look, like figures on a monument. Whether anyone ever builds them one will depend on what happens in the coming days.

A military victory is assured. But it will be for the peace, and not the fighting, that the second Gulf war will be remembered.

Seldom have democracies gone into a war in an atmosphere of such moral and logical confusion. The soldiers have stopped thinking about it and have absorbed themselves in the comforting drills and routines of their calling. The civilians in their path have no such solace. Most of the 600,000 inhabitants of Basra will remember what happened 12 years ago. After weeks of bombardment by the Allies they had to suffer the retribution of Saddam's troops who crushed the Shia uprising while the Allies stood back.

The inhabitants of the Middle East are not generally inclined to attribute positive motives to America. But a small minority of optimists are hoping that the huge effort involved in taking the path to war must be motivated by something more than American interests. Now it seems that they will find out. It is mid-afternoon now and the silence is fading. Once again, the tanks are moving up the road.

▶ Expeditionary Unit (Special Operations Capable). Commanded by Col Thomas D. Waldhauser, the 15th MEU gave Brig Dutton an additional 2,000 men, 20 armoured vehicles, including four M1A1 Abrams tanks, and the support of AH1W Super Cobra attack helicopters. Their task was to grab the oil fields at Rumaila, to prevent Saddam's henchmen from blowing the wellheads and destroying the fields.

And so, at 10pm, on a pitch-dark night, a detachment of 40 Commando, a team of US Navy Special Forces Seals and a party of Royal Navy landing strip specialists clambered into

Previous page: The body of an Iraqi lies wrapped in a blanket, a victim of the British assault on the Faw peninsula

Above: British soldiers look down at the bodies of two Iraqi soldiers, one still holding a white flag, as they lie crumpled in a trench

the MH53 Pavelow helicopter. Their task was to secure the oil facility on Faw and a landing area for the follow-on forces.

The first night of the war nearly started in disaster. The Chinook pilots had been given extensive aerial photography of the target area. One of the landing zones was on a road next to an oil spillage area. They were under strict orders not to land in the spillage area. But as the RAF pilot approached the destination, through the pale green glow of his night vision goggles he spotted something not seen on the photographs – telegraph poles.

Knowing he dare not attempt to land amid

the wires, he resorted to a novel solution. He ramped up the twin Avco Lycoming T55-712 turbo shafts that powered the 51ft helicopter to maximum power. While the scrambling Iraqi forces on the ground fired their AK47s at the hovering Chinook, the pilot used the massive downwash of the helicopter's twin 60ft rotors to blast over the poles.

Greeted by a hail of small-arms fire, the men on board scrambled out of the helicopters. The Seals dashed to their objective, securing the pumping station and pump heads and defusing Iraqi booby traps.

Any Iraqi forces that threatened them

DAY 3 22.03.03
A US marine convoy watches flames belch from a well in the Ratka oilfield, set alight by fleeing Iraqi soldiers

were met with lethal force. One six-man Seal team was reported to have killed 23 Iraqis.

As the Seals did their work, a wave of six RAF Chinooks, their pilots flying with the aid of night-vision goggles, picked up Lt Col Gordon Messenger, the commanding officer of 40 Commando, and his men. Wearing camouflage cream and carrying large Bergen packs laden with ammunition, mortar rounds and anti-tank weapons, the soldiers lined up in groups of 28 or so behind each helicopter. Once they got the radio message to go, the Chinooks took off in turn, rising gracefully and then swooping northwards and taking the

soldiers on the 20-minute trip to the Faw, where the naval airstrip experts guided in the pilots. As the Royal Marine Commandos poured into the oil facility, the Iraqis attempted to regroup and counter attack. A mortar opened up, sending some 30 rounds towards the attacking British forces.

In immediate response, Col Messenger called in artillery support from his gun line, carefully dug in on Bubiyan Island, a low-lying piece of Kuwaiti territory a short distance from Faw.

A huge firing line stretching more than four miles and consisting of British 105mm light guns and AS90 155mm self-propelled howitzers, reinforced by US Marine Corps 155mm guns, opened fire and silenced the Iraqi mortars.

In the waters of the Gulf, Marlborough, a Type 23 Frigate, and Chatham, a Type 22 Frigate, opened fire with their 4.5in naval canons in support of the attack.

While the Royal Marines fought for control of the oil terminals, coalition forces launched a number of armoured thrusts through the border.

Throughout the night of March 20 and into March 21, thousands of US forces poured into the desert wastelands of southern Iraq. Resistance was minimal as the 3rd Infantry Division crossed into Iraq at around 4.30 am local time and pushed hard and fast in a northwest direction towards the Euphrates. One US reporter described the caravan of Abrams tanks and Bradley fighting vehicles as a "huge wave of steel" that stretched for 20 miles.

At around 5am, US marines from the I Marine Expeditionary Force burst through holes cut in the border fence and headed for the oil fields. With the 63-ton Abrams tanks leading, the men in their amphibious AAA7 tracked vehicles headed for the Iraqi port of Umm Qasr. To the surprise of the attacking marines, they encountered little, if any, resistance. Two Iraqi armoured personnel carriers that were spotted close to the border were quickly destroyed.

By daybreak the US marines had stormed Umm Qasr, a vital link in coalition plans to ship much-needed aid into the country. Although they seized the port relatively quickly, the town itself proved a harder nut to crack. Determined fighters of Saddam's irregular Fedayeen were holding up in the town.

The marines were in no mood to hang around. Their business lay to the north. The plan called for the British to take control of the port to relieve the marines.

That night also saw the first casualties. In a bitter accident, a US CH46 Sea Knight helicopter crashed in the Kuwaiti desert. Alongside the four US crew, eight British ser-

vicemen – five Royal Marines, two Army gunners and a Royal Navy specialist – were killed. Mechanical failure was suspected.

Throughout the day, the attacking Allies fought a series of battles. The men of 16 Air Assault Brigade, in a *coup de main*, seized the Rumaila oilfields almost entirely intact. The Iraqis had attempted to set fire to many of the wellheads, but fewer than 10 of them were damaged before the British took control.

By daybreak, the lead elements of the US 3rd Infantry Division were reported to be 90 miles inside Iraq. In the southern Iraqi deserts they met so little resistance that by nightfall they had reached the southern city of Nasiriyah, with its strategic crossings over the Euphrates. If they could seize them intact it would be an important victory.

All through the first day of the war, thousands of aircraft rained destruction across the length of Iraq. Dug-in Iraqi troops were subjected to relentless bombardment. But for the world's observers, the air raids on Baghdad had been anti-climactic. Where was the "shock and awe" that had been promised? Where were the hundreds of satellite-guided bombs and cruise missiles that were going to cut off the head of the Iraqi regime and stun the leadership into early submission?

The doubters were to have their answers in full as Friday night fell across the Iraqi cap-

In a scene reminiscent of the First World War, a line of Iraqi prisoners of war is evacuated from the Faw peninsula by US marines with 40 Commando

ital. Ominously air raid sirens sounded at about 8.09pm, but the first strikes were visible only as dozens of flashes in the distance. Less than an hour later, the full brunt of America's ire struck at the heart of Baghdad.

From one side of the city to the other came the thunder of crashing glass as shock waves swept across the Tigris in both directions. Some 300 cruise missiles came in low and fast, striking with truly awesome precision. Saddam's main presidential palace, on the banks of the Tigris, was engulfed in a cauldron of fire.

At least five missiles struck the nearby headquarters of Special Security, the fearsome domestic intelligence agency. The Republican Guard's HQ was also struck, as was the Rashid Barracks, a military camp on Baghdad's southern outskirts. The office of Tariq Aziz, the deputy prime minister, was razed.

After the missiles came waves of aircraft. Building after building was engulfed in fire and smoke as the heart of Saddam's regime was pulverised and destroyed. In a three-hour blitz that at times brought a new blast every 10 seconds the city was rocked with explosions.

And finally, when the bombing stopped, under a full moon, the fires burned. If there was any doubt of what Iraq was about to endure, it had been fully laid to rest. This would be a war unlike any other.

'THIS IS GOING TO GET A LOT HARDER'

The war was going well. Allied tanks were charging north at speed towards Baghdad, and Basra looked ready to fall. But suddenly a series of tragic accidents and some unexpected resistance changed the mood…

US marines from the 2nd Battalion, 8th Regiment, on the outskirts of Basra, show the scars of battle

DAY 4 23.03.03 Royal Marines from 40 Commando take aim against enemy positions during street fighting on the Faw peninsula

Black smoke spews from one of the blazing oil trenches that circle Baghdad, casting a pall to disrupt allied air strikes

As Gen Tommy Franks, the US commander of Operation Iraqi Freedom, stood in front of the world's press at the hi-tech media centre at Centcom HQ in Doha, Qatar, on the morning of Saturday, March 22, he could be forgiven if he felt pretty good about things.

The US 3rd Infantry Division was at that very moment executing the fastest armoured advance in the history of modern warfare. The British, backed up by US marines, had grabbed almost intact the oil facilities in the south of the country, and had under their control almost half of oil-rich Iraq's reserves. Baghdad, the Iraqi capital, had been subjected to an awe-inspiring bombardment of unprecedented accuracy – even the Iraqis admitted that only three people were killed in the three-hour blitz – and the US marines had taken the strategic port of Umm Qasr and were in the

Right: An Iraqi, head bowed, sits in blood-stained clothes, awaiting medical help for shrapnel wounds after being caught in fighting near Basra

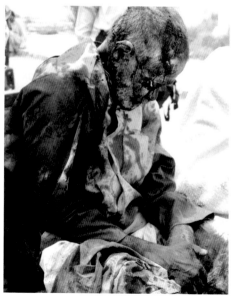

process of fighting through the town to secure it. It was, all things considered, about the best start to a war any general could ask for. But it was quickly apparent to the 58-year-old Franks that it was not a view widely shared by the assembled media.

He had a tough act to follow. In 1991 General "Stormin' Norman" Schwarzkopf, the larger-than-life commander of Centcom, had more than filled the room. Gen Franks lacked his charisma. His performance that Saturday was shaky, and lacked conviction. "This will be a campaign unlike any other in history," he told the journalists. He was right, but not entirely in ways he could have predicted.

The opening questions, from the US broadcast media, were gentle enough, but when journalists from the rest of the world pitched in, it soon became clear to the general that he was fighting two wars simultaneously –

Above: Having pushed halfway to Baghdad in record time, US marines stop to round up a party of surrendering Iraqi soldiers near the town of Az Bayr

one brilliantly in the sands of Iraq, the other, a far more unpredictable battle, on the screens and pages of the world's media. Despite the initial successes of the ground war, it seemed that the media war was beginning to slip through the allies' fingers.

Britain had already lost eight men in that helicopter crash in Kuwait. Disaster struck again. Two Royal Navy Sea King Mk 7 Airborne Early Warning helicopters collided at sea about five miles out from the British air-craft carrier Ark Royal. All seven men, one US serviceman, and six Royal Navy lieutenants, all from 849 Squadron based at RNAS Culdrose, were killed. The youngest, Marc Lawrence, was just 26. Niggling doubts began to be asked about Britain's preparedness.

The uneasiness was increased when news broke that three ITN journalists, including the veteran war reporter Terry Lloyd, ▶46

Iraqis cheer as soldiers search the banks of the Tigris for a US pilot mistakenly thought to have parachuted from his downed jet

An Iraqi T55 tank dug into the sand outside Basra lies abandoned after being destroyed by heavy shelling

An Iraqi claiming to have shot down a US Apache helicopter near Karbala using only a rifle enjoys his moment of fame

Baghdad is blacked out as Saddam's troops extend the use of blazing oil pits as a primitive air defence

▶ were missing in southern Iraq after coming under fire near Basra. There were reports that the men had been shot at not by Iraqis, but by Allied troops. Worse was to come that night. The radar screen in the Engagement Control Station of a Patriot missile battery guarding the air base at Ali al Saleem flashed an incoming track. Within a fraction of a second, the multi-million-pound system classified the track as not friendly and immediately plotted for intercept. The US female lieutenant commander had only seconds to decide: was it an Iraqi incoming attack, maybe another Scud launch, or was it a coalition aircraft not responding as it should? She could take no chances. She fired.

In the air, a formation of Tornados, their mission accomplished, was returning to base. Ground crew were waiting on the flight line to see the aircraft back.

As the two aircraft neared the base in the

Jessica Lynch: the 19-year-old was one of six Americans from a 507th Maintenance Company team captured by Iraqis on Day 3. Seven of her comrades were killed in the engagement

dark skies, warning alarms suddenly went off inside the Tornado GR4 of Wing Commander Derek Watson. He was under surface-to-air missile attack. Immediately, years of training cut in as almost by instinct he took evasive action. He launched chaff and flares to distract the missile and, as he radioed a warning to his wingman, he saw a fireball as the missile sped at five times the speed of sound over his aircraft.

For the second Tornado there was to be no escape. The 5.2m missile smashed into the aircraft. Its 75kg warhead detonated, tearing the plane apart. The pilot, Flight Lieutenant Kevin Barry Main, and his navigator, Flight Lieutenant David Rhys Williams, both from IX(B) Squadron, were killed almost certainly instantly.

Another disaster was to follow. At 1am local time on Sunday, the stillness of the Kuwaiti night was shattered. Inside the

perimeter of the tented camp of a brigade of the 101st Airborne Division came two grenade blasts followed by a burst of automatic fire. Sentries dashed to the scene of the explosions – the tents housing the commanders and senior staff officers – expecting to find Iraqi Special Forces. What they found proved even more shocking. The attacker, it appeared, was one of their own men. A Muslim sergeant serving with the division had apparently disabled a generator, and then in the darkness tossed a grenade into each tent before pumping rounds through the canvas. Army Captain Christopher Scott Seifert, 27, died immediately. Fifteen others were injured.

There was better news from the battlefield. In Umm Qasr, British and US forces continued to wheedle out the last remaining pockets of resistance. And in the vast expanse of the southern Iraqi desert, American ground forces continued their dramatic advance. As

DAY 4 24.03.03

Below: British soldiers from 29 Commando Regiment Royal Artillery fire salvos from their 105mm guns during the push north

they pushed harder and harder towards the heart of the regime, Baghdad, the 3rd US Infantry Division covered more ground in one day than the American divisions of the 1991 Gulf war covered in four.

By mid-afternoon on Sunday March 23, reporters travelling with the division's second brigade were only 150 miles from Baghdad. Since crossing the border some 40 hours earlier, the division had covered 228 miles and were fast approaching the town of Najaf.

Following behind was the I Marine Expeditionary Force. Gen Franks ordered his US marines to grab the bridges at Nasiriyah, cross the Euphrates and then push north-west in a two-prong advance. The western advance should head towards the town of Diwaniyah, the eastern due north to Kut on the Tigris.

But as they approached Nasiriyah, they ran into resistance. Members of the Fedayeen, paramilitaries loyal to the Ba'ath Party, ▶64

DAY 5 25.03.03
Previous page: Royal
Marines Omar Rawlings,
left, and Del Morton see
the funny side as they
are forced to squeeze
into their dugout. Heavy
rain north of the Faw
peninsula had turned the
desert into a quagmire

Right: A sand-coated US
army combat engineer
tries to make radio
contact at a checkpoint
between Najaf and
Karbala as a sandstorm
turns the daylight orange

US marines help a wounded colleague despite being under intense enemy fire during skirmishes outside Nasiriyah

DESPATCH
22.03.03 FROM PATRICK BISHOP IN BASRA
DIEHARDS KEEP ALLIES AT BAY

The biblical landscape of southern Iraq was crowded with the fighting machinery of the 21st century yesterday. But despite the massive technological advantages of the Allies, progress was slow in subduing a region that was meant to fold at the first push.

According to the script, the process of liberating Basra should have been well under way by now. The fighting was supposed to have finished and a *modus vivendi* established with the local authorities as the first aid shipments docked.

Instead, the sun-baked khaki plain before the city echoed intermittently with the sound of bombs, shells and missiles as the Allies' attempts to extinguish the last embers of resistance continued. In the deep-water port of Umm Qasr, a group of hold-outs were blasted with two 500lb bombs in an attempt to dislodge them.

In Basra, which the military authorities are anxious to secure without a full-scale fight, there were more aerial attacks to dislodge what were described as "militiamen" – groups hiding among the several hundred thousand, mostly Shi'ite, population and apparently trying to lure the British 7th Armoured Brigade into a street battle.

There is no doubt that most of the soldiers sent by Saddam Hussein to defend Basra want peace as fast as possible. "They don't want to shoot at us and we don't want to shoot at them," said one British officer.

A group of prisoners huddled in blankets at the roadside after surrendering radiated relief as they wolfed their US ration packs and drank bottled water. "America is good," they yelled. "Saddam is finished," adding, with their eyes rolled upwards, a fervent "Thanks be to God". The military and civilian authorities in Basra seem eager to fall in with the allies' plan to arrange a local ceasefire to allow normalisation to begin and free the military thrust to sweep quickly upcountry to Baghdad.

But the local people have learned to be suspicious of everyone. Behind each smile and wave is a thick wall of wariness. Everyone remembers the last time, 12 years ago, when the Americans seemed to be coming to help but stood by and let the uprising they had encouraged be crushed by Saddam. The sooner the aid is flowing and the shooting stops, the faster trust can be built. That is being frustrated by small groups of zealots whose motivations are unknown but who seem determined to fight to the death. Even the most optimistic forecasts predicted some bumps on the road to Baghdad. But the obstacles came sooner than expected. The question is whether this is just an initial local difficulty or a warning of bigger problems ahead.

The body of a US marine, ambushed in Nasiriyah, hangs from his vehicle while, right, prayers are said for Capt Christopher Seifert

In the back of a Toyota pick-up, an Iraqi woman lets out a wail of despair as she and her family flee fighting on the road to Basra

Saved for a rainy day: An umbrella proves useful as a deluge falls on the British Support Group camp outside Basra

Sitting out the storm: With faces wrapped in scarves, two US troops endure a sandstorm near Karbala that was to delay progress north

Base camp: American marines try to make themselves at home in a field of mud outside Nasiriyah after heavy storms

The bog of war: a member of the Queens Dragoon Guards puts his feet up in the rain-lashed desert

DESPATCH

26.03.03 FROM TIM BUTCHER
IN UMM QASR

DOLPHINS CALLED IN TO HUNT FOR MINES

A bottle-nosed dolphin with a search device attached to its flipper leaps from the water during a training session in the Gulf

Makai and Tacoma, two bottlenose Atlantic dolphins, were flown into Iraq by the United States navy last night, the latest weapon deployed by allied forces against Saddam Hussein.

The specially-trained dolphins will start work today, searching for mines in the approaches to the port of Umm Qasr so that a safe route can be created for shipments of humanitarian aid into southern Iraq.

Scores of mines, including Italian-made Manta mines – which detonate when they pick up magnetic or acoustic signals – have been found still on Iraqi ships but it is feared others may have already been sown.

As part of the US navy's secret Marine Mammal Project, the dolphins have been trained to use their in-built sonar – the clicking that humans can hear – to locate mines, which they then mark with floats. They are taught to avoid touching the mines, which might cause the devices to explode, and Capt Mike Tillotson, a US navy bomb disposal expert, said there was no significant risk to the animals in doing this work.

The biggest hazard could come from other indigenous dolphins in the waters of Umm Qasr. Dolphins, he explained, are territorial and there is a fear that local dolphins might drive away the incomers, causing them to go Awol.

"They are like children really," said Petty Officer Taylor Whitaker, 23, Tacoma's handler. "They are keen and work very hard but sometimes they can have a bad day. Tacoma is one of the most vocal ones we have and one of the best at his job."

Although the US navy has been working on the dolphin mine-searching programme for years, this is its first operational deployment. An earlier US project, using dolphins to protect warships by butting enemy divers, was used in the 1960s in Vietnam and during the Cold War the Soviet Union trained dolphins to plant limpet mines on enemy vessels. The US navy has more than 20 dolphins on the programme, based in San Diego, California,

and nine have been flown out to the Gulf for the war on Iraq. They have spent the past few weeks on board a US warship in special tanks. Tacoma, a 22-year-old male, and Makai, a 33-year-old male, were flown forward by helicopter yesterday on special travelling sleeves, doused with water, to the port at Umm Qasr. Today they will start sweeping the waters by the dockside.

US warships suffered two mine strikes during the last Gulf war and intelligence pictures over the past few months showed intense Iraqi naval activity in Umm Qasr.

Small patrol boats had canvas covers erected over their sterns and once Allied forces entered the port they found the covers concealed rails used to deploy mines. One boat laden with mines was found submerged next to a jetty, possibly as a booby trap. More worryingly, a customised barge with more than 90 mines on board was found near Umm Qasr. The hold had been re-engineered to deploy mines which would be invisible to US spy planes. There is a worry the barge has already deployed some of the weapons.

Above: A British Warrior armoured vehicle shows its contempt for Iraq's dictator by pushing over a mural in Basra depicting him in military fatigues

Left: Desert Rats, members of Zulu Company, pose with a portrait of Saddam that was liberated from the Ba'ath Party headquarters in Basra

An Iraqi runs past the
burning shells of cars
destroyed when a missile
struck a market-place
in northern Baghdad.
Twelve people died
in the explosion

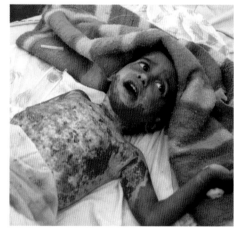

Top: British troops with medical supplies visit a mother and baby in Basra

Above left: Bodies lie by the road after a coach carrying Republican Guards was fired on

Left: An Iraqi solder, killed in a gun battle, lies slumped in the back of a blood-caked minivan

Above: A child, burned in allied air strikes on Baghdad, awaits treatment

Right: A child, caught in fighting, is helped away by a US soldier

▶ opened fire, blasting them with mortars, RPG7 anti-tank weapons and .50cal machine guns mounted on pick-up trucks. This was fighting of a ferocity unseen so far on the battlefield.

The Fedayeen resorted to any tactic in their bid to stop the marines. One group, dressed in civilian clothes, appeared to surrender. But it was a trap. As the marines went forward, they were cut down in a hail of gunfire. Nine marines died, the largest loss of life so far in combat.

Further tragedy was to blight the Americans in Nasiriyah. A team from the 507th Maintenance Company, attempting to drive around the town, took a wrong turning. They drove straight into a hailstorm of AK47 and RPG7 fire. The US soldiers – mechanics, clerks and cooks – were outgunned and outnumbered. Despite overwhelming odds, they fought on, killing several attackers. But their plight was hopeless. Fifteen minutes later seven Americans lay dead. The other six, some badly wounded, surrendered. Among the six were two women, Shoshana Nyree Johnson, a 30-year-old single mother from El Paso, Texas, and a 19-year-old private first class from West Virginia. Her name: Jessica Lynch.

Hours later, the world knew of their fate. Harrowing pictures of the traumatised soldiers were transmitted around the world. Johnson, the only woman on the video, held her arms tightly across her chest and appeared terrified – her wide eyes darting to and fro. A laughing Iraqi could be heard taunting the Americans: "You expected to be met with flowers, didn't you?" The station also broadcast footage of grinning Iraqis next to what appeared to be American corpses – killed, said the Iraqi commentator, at Nasiriyah.

Speaking at the evening press conference at the Pentagon, Gen Myers, the US Chairman of the Joint Chiefs of Staff, commented of the Iraqis, "Clearly they are not a beaten force. This is going to get a lot harder."

He was right. On Monday, March 24, an attack formation of 40 AH64D Apache Longbow helicopters from the 11th Aviation Regiment took to the air. Like giant insects slowly they lifted up, turned north and sped away to strike the tanks of the Medina division of the Republican Guard.

But as the low-flying helicopters approached Iraqi tank targets near Hillah, 60 miles south of Baghdad, Iraqi troops in a palm-lined residential area let loose a sheet of fire from anti-aircraft guns, rocket-propelled grenades, rifles and other small arms. ▶70

DAY 8 27.03.03
Above: On the canal bridge out of Basra, Iraqi refugees, fleeing Saddam's supporters in the city, pass others trying to return to obtain news of missing relatives

Left: US soldiers place a blanket over the body of an Iraqi soldier killed in a battle to secure a bridge over the Euphrates

Right: Exuberant Iraqi youngsters accompany a British Marine from 42 Commando as he patrols the southern town of Um Qa-eel

Next page: A Royal Marine is engulfed in smoke a split second after firing off a Milan wire-guided missile at an enemy position on the Faw Peninsula

▶ "It was like a hornet's nest out there," one pilot, Doug Sanders, said later. At least 30 of the $25m helicopters were heavily damaged and had to return to base. One went down, and its two-man crew, Chief Warrant Officer David Williams, 30, and Chief Warrant Officer Ronald Young Jr, 26, was captured. Within hours, they, too, were paraded for the Iraqi cameras. A television newscaster interviewed a farmer who claimed to have shot down the helicopter with an old hunting rifle. Standing beside the wreckage he waved the gun in the air, making the most of his moment of fame.

It began to appear that the allies might have miscalculated. Far from being only too willing to surrender, some Iraqis were putting up quite dogged resistance.

"Cakewalk theory" pundits embedded in television studios on both sides of the Atlantic were quickly replaced by "quagmire analysts": frequently the same experts reversing their previous line, switching roles with ease .

British casualties, too, began to mount. Two members of 33 Engineer Regiment (EOD) – Sapper Luke Allsopp, 24, from North London and Staff Sergeant Simon Cullingworth, 36, from Essex – went missing after their convoy was attacked near Basra.

Despite gains, the tenacity of Iraqi resistance and mounting casualties gave fuel to critics. Lt Gen William S Wallace, the US army's senior ground commander in Iraq, spoke with a candor that embarrassed his superiors. "The enemy we're fighting is different from the one we had war-gamed against," he said.

As the initiative continued to eke away from the allies, a sandstorm of biblical proportions swept central Iraq. The air literally became blood red. Visibility was slashed to a few yards. Stinging sand cut the soldiers' faces. Men from the 3rd Infantry Division huddled inside their Bradley fighting vehicles, tying ropes around their waists whenever they dared to venture outside.

A soldier with the 101st Airborne Division's 3rd Brigade left his tent to go to a latrine only a few yards away. He was lost for eight hours in winds whipping at more than 50mph. Allied convoys took 27 hours to make a trip that should have taken 12 hours at the most. "The second sign of the Apocalypse," was one soldier's description of the storm.

For the US marines still fighting to secure the bridges at Nasiriyah, the sandstorms only added to their problems. For three days they fought running battles with the Fedayeen,

Previous page: A soldier walks beneath the barrels of Challenger 2 tanks from Britain's 7th Armoured Brigade after a victorious encounter with Iraqi T55s

who, despite the overwhelming firepower of the I Marine Expeditionary Force, managed to block the advance north. Some analysts sharply criticised the war plan, saying it did not include enough troops to do the job. Irritated Bush administration officials began to lash out. "This isn't a matter of timetable, it's a matter of victory," Mr Bush said.

The media briefers went on the attack. They pointed to the massive aerial bombardment that continued round the clock, despite the weather – some 1,400 sorties against the Republican Guard alone in one 24-hour period. But even the air strikes could not remain immune to the storm. A dozen aircraft from the USS Harry S Truman, sailing in the

Above: An American Abrams tank charges northwards, part of the allies' record-breaking dash to Baghdad

Mediterranean, took off on bombing runs but were forced to return a few hours later.

Though much of the media concentrated on the setbacks, the enhanced sense of doom obscured the truth that the allies were making excellent progress in their advances towards Basra and Baghdad, and in the largely unseen and forgotten northern front, on the border with Kurdish-held northern Iraq. An unsteady peace had existed in northern Iraq since the 1991 Gulf war and the establishment of UN safe havens to protect the Kurdish majority. The Kurds were bitter opponents of Saddam, and in them Gen Franks saw a useful ally. When his plans to open a second front against Baghdad through Turkey were thwarted by Ankara, he hoped to use the fearsome Kurdish fighters, the peshmerga, to take on the Iraqis in the north.

Also, northern Iraq held nearly half of the country's oil fields, near the two strategic towns of Kirkuk and Mosul. The Iraqi defenders of the two towns had been subjected to devastating air attacks from the outset of the war.

Desperate to relieve pressure on his troops in the south and to open a second front in the north, Gen Franks called up the 173rd Airborne Brigade, a specialist parachute unit based in Europe.

The 1,000-man brigade clambered aboard the giant C17 Globemaster transport planes in Vincenza, Italy, and, over Kurdish-held northern Iraq, made the first parachute drop by US troops since the 1989 invasion of Panama. It was a clear sign to the Iraqis: we are coming at you from all angles.

While the sandstorms ravaged central Iraq, the British in the south continued to mop up pockets of resistance in Umm Qasr, before switching their attention to Iraq's second city, Basra. The move on the Shia-dominated city had already claimed its first casualty, Britain's first combat death of the war.

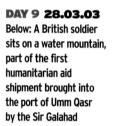

DAY 9 28.03.03

Below: A British soldier sits on a water mountain, part of the first humanitarian aid shipment brought into the port of Umm Qasr by the Sir Galahad

When Sgt Stephen Mark Roberts, 33, from Bradford and serving with 2nd Royal Tank Regiment, rolled into the town of Zubayr, in his 70-ton Challenger 2 tank his crew drove straight into a riot.

In a selfless act that was to cost him his life, Sgt Roberts did what any British soldier would have tried to do – sort it out peacefully. Leaving the safety of his tank, he clambered down and began to talk to the crowd. As he did so he was shot dead by a sniper.

The move on the city was to cost two more British lives in an accident. In the early hours of Tuesday, March 25, two soldiers with the Queen's Royal Lancers, Cpl Stephen John Allbutt, from Stoke-on-Trent, and Tpr David Jeffrey Clarke, from Littleworth, Staffordshire, died when their Challenger 2 tank was hit by another. The force of the depleted uranium high-velocity armour-piercing round smashing into the Challenger at

more than 1,500 metres per second took the 20-ton turret off the tank. Two other soldiers on board were seriously injured.

It fell to the British to help the allies regain the momentum and stem the flow of bad news. While the Americans had been pushing north into the heart of Iraq, the British had been fighting their own battles. The Challenger 2 tanks and Warrior armoured infantry vehicles of 7th Armoured Brigade, the "Desert Rats", had pushed hard from the Kuwaiti border and were in positions around Basra, Iraq's sprawling second city; the more lightly equipped 3 Commando Brigade was moving up from the south to take up blocking positions.

Major Gen Robin Brims, Britain's senior Army commander in the field, planned to lay siege to the city. He hoped that by blocking it off, the pressure inside would mount to bursting point and the city would collapse from

Above: Members of RAF 617 squadron, the 'Dambusters', pose for a group portrait on the 60th anniversary of the squadron's formation. Its crews had been flying bombing missions over Iraq from the Ali al Saleem airbase in Kuwait

within. Gen Franks, back in Qatar, watched with interest. If it worked in Basra, the allied command believed, it would work in Baghdad.

At first, it appeared that the plan was working. As the British took up positions around the city, first a trickle, and then a torrent of refugees began to flood down the city's main highways.

But Saddam's men were not beaten. If proof were needed of the cruelty that the inhabitants of the city had endured under 30 years of tyranny, it was played out in front of the frustrated British troops.

The Fedayeen, holed up in Basra, began to mortar the fleeing refugees, killing scores and injuring many more. The heavy guns of 3rd Royal Horse Artillery responded, sending dozens of lethal 155mm rounds into their positions. And on Wednesday, March 26, the British had their greatest battle of the war to date. Just before dawn, a heavy fog lay across

the city. There had been sporadic shelling through the night and the British forces were on full alert. Suddenly, observation posts in the south reported hearing armour moving. Moments later they saw them – a column of Iraqi tanks, mainly T55s moving fast due south, heading for the Faw peninsula. Was this a counter attack or desertion?

An Iraqi prisoner of war who has been shot in the chest is flown to a field hospital in a British Puma helicopter

Brig Jim Dutton didn't waste time trying to find out. Mustering the anti-tank weapons under his control – mainly the Milan missile – the Marines attacked. But it soon became apparent that the threat was more significant than first thought. Once again the firepower of the AS90 155mm howitzers of 3 Regiment, Royal Horse Artillery, proved deadly.

But it was airpower that stopped the attack dead in its tracks. US F15 and F16s and British Harriers were on call and pounded the column relentlessly. That, combined with sweeping attacks by attack helicopters, left 19 Iraqi T55s burning in a Basra field.

Meanwhile, it appeared there was a second column of some 14 T55s attempting to break out. C squadron of the Royal Scots Dragoon Guards, under the command of Major Johnny Biggart, counter-attacked. Crashing across sodden marsh ground, the Challenger 2 tanks fired their deadly 120mm guns while charging at full speed. In just a few seconds the 14 Iraqi tanks were annihilated. The battle for Basra had begun.

Top left: After days of sandstorms, the sun sets in a clear sky as US M9-A1 tanks take up position near Karbala

Left: Flames light up the desert as a US M109 artillery vehicle opens fire during fierce fighting north of Najaf

Top right: The body of an Iraqi soldier lies in the baked desert sand as a convoy of US marines drives past

Above: the shells of US vehicles lie smoking after being destroyed by friendly fire. Some 37 US soldiers were wounded

A group of Iraqi civilians, fear showing in their faces, throw themselves to the ground as mortar shells fall nearby during fighting in Basra

Smoke from a burning
oil well blackens the
evening sky over empty
marshland south of Basra

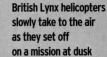
British Lynx helicopters slowly take to the air as they set off on a mission at dusk

PART THREE: MARCH 29-APRIL 5

'AMERICA DOESN'T LEAVE ITS HEROES BEHIND'

After their biggest battle yet, US tank crews paused for breath. At a checkpoint, an explosion raised the daunting spectre of suicide attacks. Then, out of the blue, an Iraqi lawyer provided an amazing tip-off . . .

Lt Col Richard Watts, fourth right, keeps staff up to date with an attack on an Iraqi-held position during a briefing inside the Command Post at 3 Commando HQ

The winds of change began to blow through the allied campaign. The biting sandstorms started to abate. But the sand had not brought the war to a halt. It just made the unbearable even worse. The fighting carried on.

At Nasiriyah the US marines eventually broke through. Although the city was far from secured, Lt Gen James Conway, commanding general of the I Marine Exditionary Force, took a risk. As long as he owned the bridges, he could get forces through the city and carry on the attack north, leaving other troops behind to mop up the city.

It fell to the 3rd Battalion, 1st Marine Regiment to lead the way. The bridges on either end of the city were secure, but a two-mile stretch right through the middle of Nasiriyah was still in Iraqi hands. The marines called it Sniper Alley.

As the troops prepared to move, the warning was blunt: "This is a gauntlet, men," said Capt Matt Reid, a company commander. "This is what it's all about. If you ever thought you weren't going into combat in the Marine Corps you were wrong. We're friggin' gonna' run the gauntlet."

The leading tanks rolled into town just after 11pm. Within seconds of reaching the far side of the bridge they came under fire. Capt Reid gave the order, "Weapons free" – the marine's way of saying, "Shoot anything that moves." And they did. The lines of houses that faced the road on either side were demolished. Mud bricks and plaster crumbled under the marines' constant fire. Flames engulfed homes

DAY 10 29.03.03

Left: An Iraqi woman gestures to a Marine as she stares down the barrel of his gun while he scans the street for enemy forces

Previous page: A vast scrapyard of rusting metal stretching across the desert is pictured from an allied plane seeking Iraqi missiles

blasted with anti-armour rounds. Mortars were fired at dangerously close range to take out snipers. A broken water main pump flooded the rubble of a demolished corner house.

But the marines got through. The last units of the miles-long convoy passed in the morning of Tuesday, March 25, After moving beyond Nasiriyah, the 1st Marine Regiment crawled north, advancing as far as Qal'at Sukkar by Thursday, after taking only isolated sniper and mortar fire.

Meanwhile, on the west bank of the Euphrates, the vanguard of the American thrust was 3rd Squadron, 7th Cavalry. Their mission was to act as forward guard for the entire 3rd Infantry Division. If something was out there, they found it. The army call it reconnaissance by firepower, the military equivalent of lobbing stones at wasps' nests. If the other side shoots back, then you know where they are. "Cav" find the enemy, others deal with them. It was a battle plan that had stood the 3/7th Cavalry well.

Top: Two Iraqi boys get themselves in the picture as a heavily armed British Marine patrols the streets of Umm Qasr

Above: An Iraq woman carries home a box of supplies delivered to Safwan by a Red Crescent convoy

The initial plan at Nasiriyah had been for the 3rd Infantry Division to take the city, which the allies believed would be welcoming them, if not quite with garlands, then at least with a quick surrender. When it became clear that this was not going to be the case, the plan changed. The 3rd Division was eventually told to leave the battle to the US marines, and to push on north, the 3/7th leading the way.

At the next town on the road to the Baghdad, Samawah, the squadron was better prepared. At 8.30pm Monday, March 24, 200 Iraqi troops lit up the night with small arms and machinegun fire. Red tracers arched back and forth as the enemy traded shots with the Cavalry troops firing 7.62mm machineguns on their tanks and Bradleys.

Lt Col Terry Ferrell, the squadron commander, called on his six M109A6 Paladin 155mm self-propelled howitzers to fire one round each at the Iraqi positions. Moments later, six orange fireballs exploded over the enemy positions; they fell silent. At about ▶98

Above: British troops are forced to push back crowds of Iraqis amid chaotic scenes as the first deliveries of humanitarian aid arrive in the southern town of Zubaya

Left: The coffin of one of the British fallen is carried from a transport plane after touching down at RAF Brize Norton

Battle ready: A campaign portrait of the 1st Battalion Parachute Regiment

DESPATCH

02.04.03 FROM PATRICK BISHOP
ART OF WINNING HEARTS AND MINDS

As I write this, the sound of bagpipes is drifting across the desert. It should seem incongruous, but in a funny way it doesn't. This dusty corner of Iraq has heard the skirl before. The names of the dead of the Scottish regiments killed in the 1914-21 campaign are inscribed on tablets in the memorial that stands, strangely intact, only a mile or so from here.

Nearly two weeks into the campaign, the Brits are managing somehow to fit in to Iraq. It's hot and dirty, there's no beer and not all the natives are friendly. But they will make the best of it – "crack on", as everyone around here says.

The same cannot be claimed for the Americans. The further they advance, the less comfortable they seem with their surroundings, a condition that can have terrible results, as the killing of women and children at a checkpoint shows.

It is often the case in war that allies look askance at each other. But considering the British and American armies as they pursue Saddam, one is still struck by the differences in the way that they go to war. The styles and attitudes are so distinct as to sometimes make it seem remarkable that they manage to be allies.

The impression the American forces give as they thunder up Route Tampa towards Baghdad is that everyone outside their ranks is a potential enemy: certainly the awe-struck peasants whose nervous waves are met with blank stares; and possibly the "unilateral" independent news teams whose pleas for food, fuel and shelter are brusquely rejected.

Indeed, anyone who is not in a uniform that they instantly recognise is seen as a threat. British troops, by contrast, seem remarkably well disposed towards the Iraqis, even though among those smiling and cadging cigarettes are men who would be happy to kill them. The confidence-building got off to a slow start. Then, as always, it was the children who came forward first. Now the gates of the bases in Umm Qasr and Zubayr have a permanent throng of the curious, the friendly and the importuning, just as they did in Bosnia and Kosovo.

British troops seem to have a natural sympathy for the poor foreigners they habitually find themselves having to sort out and a mild interest in the political and cultural forces that created the mess. If they are in a place long enough, they play football with the local men and sleep with and sometimes marry their sisters.

The right and wrongs of the situation may be of less concern now

that the war has started, than the result of the Ireland-England rugby game. That is not to say that they don't have their own opinions, usually shrewd when expressed and laced with a genial cynicism that would dismay Tony Blair.

The American troops whom I have come across appear uninterested in their immediate surroundings. They do, though, pay attention to their leader and seem to accept the White House version of what this is all about. They talk without embarrassment about honour and duty. The boys from the Mersey and the Thames and the Tyne feel these things as profoundly as any American, but they would die of shame before they uttered the words.

They look on their allies with a mixture of alarm and condescension. The Septics, as the Cockneys call them, are often the first suspects when there is news of casualties. The Brits distrust their reliance on technology and laugh – though perhaps not without envy – at their superabundance of kit.

Many feel disquiet at the massive use of force that seems to accompany the most minor operations. Last week, British troops watched with horrified fascination as an empty building near Umm Qasr, which sketchy reports said may have contained a handful of Saddam's men, was bombed and rocketed continuously for several hours.

The American military's awkwardness with the people it finds itself among used to be blamed on its lack of experience in messy, complicated places such as Northern Ireland. But that has not been the case for some time. American troops went into Bosnia in 1995 as peacekeepers and later to Kosovo. In both deployments there was minimal contact with the locals.

The American soldiers' conduct is the consequence of a doctrine that puts the security of the military force at the forefront of all thought and action. In practice, this means having as little to do as possible with civilians.

Many, probably most, Iraqis are willing to be persuaded that the Americans are in their country as liberators, not invaders.

To do that, American soldiers have to not only curb their trigger-happy ways, but also come out from behind their Ray-Bans. They should learn to wave at the children and say hello in Arabic to their elders. In short, they must work harder to show that they belong to the human race.

They do not have to look far to see how this is done. They are sitting alongside the most professional and humane army on earth. Britain's contribution in men and weapons to the campaign may not be large enough to give us much say in how the fighting is done. But the weight we bring to the effort to persuade Iraqis not to hate us is enormous.

Kuwaiti firemen fight to cap a blazing well in the Rumaila oilfields after it was set alight by retreating Iraqi forces

▶ 9.30pm the Cavalry rolled out. The biggest battles still lay ahead, as the 3rd Infantry approached the city of Najaf.

The site of the tomb of the Iman Ali, son-in-law of the Prophet Mohammed, the city is one of the holiest sites in the Shia faith. Allied intelligence had described it as a hotbed of anti-Saddamism, but they had said the same of most of the south. Gen Buford C Blount III, the commanding general of 3rd Infantry Division, was not going to risk his men's lives on the strength of questionable intelligence.

The city of more than 100,000 people, about 85 miles south of Baghdad, was not even one of the general's military objectives.

The battle around Najaf, the division's most intense in six days of fighting, began late

Previous page: People leaving Basra are frisked by British soldiers after claims that some troops loyal to Saddam were donning civilian clothing in an attempt to slip through checkpoints

on Monday night. The US 3rd Infantry Division's First Brigade had made its own way to a spot south of the city directly from the Kuwaiti border. It now sent a tank company across a bridge north of Najaf, with the intent of blocking the main roads into the city from the north. This was the first time the division's troops had crossed the Euphrates.

The 3/7th Cavalry captured a bridge south of the city late the next day, while the First Brigade seized another northern bridge, effectively completing the encirclement of Najaf.

However, Gen Franks was determined not to allow the advance to get bogged down in street fighting. He ordered elements of the US 3rd Infantry Division to "screen off" Najaf, trapping the fighters in the city, while the rest

of the division prepared for their next objective, Karbala.

Karbala marked the outer ring of the so-called Red Zone – the defences of Baghdad. It marked the point at which the Americans would encounter the Republican Guard.

By the low standards of the Iraqi army, the Republican Guard was an elite. Overseen by Saddam's son, Qusay, its 70,000 men, mainly minority Sunni Muslims, were better trained, better paid, housed in better quarters and better disciplined than the rest of the Iraqi army. Most importantly, none were conscripts.

Kitted out with the best equipment Iraq could offer – although hopelessly outgunned by the British and US – the forces comprised six divisions: three armoured, each with about

A father carries his child in search of safety as they leave the heavy fighting and acrid smoke of a blazing Basra

250 tanks, and 150 APCs; two mechanised infantry, each with about 150 T72 tanks, and about 300 armoured personnel carriers; and one lighter infantry, mainly truck-mounted troops. The heroic names of some of the divisions underscored their elite character: Nebuchadnezzar, the second and greatest king of the Chaldean dynasty of Babylonia known for his military might; Hammurabi, the most renowned ruler of the Amorite dynasty of Babylon; and Medina, celebrated as the place from which Muhammad conquered all of Arabia after his flight from Mecca. Behind the grandiose names, lay a very different reality.

The Republican Guard knew only too well the destructive firepower of the US army. In the 1991 Gulf war a single battalion ▶102

DAY 11 30.03.03

Exodus: As fighting continues to drag on in Basra, the people of the city continue to flee however they can. The children, above, have been consigned to the boot. British patrols, right, are constantly on the alert for snipers and even children come under scrutiny at checkpoints. Left, an Iraqi with a giant packet of cigarettes attracts attention but is apparently just a heavy smoker

▶ of 50 US tanks wiped out an entire brigade of the Republican Guard, destroying 76 T72 tanks, 95 armoured personnel carriers, eight artillery guns and a myriad of trucks, within hours.

To the south of Baghdad were the main forces: the Nebuchadnezzar mechanised infantry division, and in the path of the advancing 3rd Infantry Division, the Medina armoured division. To the south-east the Baghdad mechanised division had taken up a blocking position. The three other divisions were in defensive positions around the city. The Adnan mechanised infantry was close

Life goes on in Baghdad below an oily blanket of smoke as people take advantage of a lull in allied air strikes to go about their business

into Baghdad in the north, the Al Nida armoured division was to the north-east of the city, and the Hammurabi armoured due west.

With most of the rest of the division embroiled in the fight round Najaf, the 3/7th pushed north. As they approached the city amid a swirling sandstorm, they were attacked by wave after wave of Fedayeen irregulars.

The onslaught proved pitiful. The attackers were mown down in sheets of machine gun fire. The pick-up trucks, with machine guns mounted on the back, stood no chance against even the 25mm cannon on the Bradley, to say nothing of the 120mm main gun of the world's

most sophisticated tank, the Abrams. According to US reports, up to 1,000 Fedayeen were killed. It was not a battle. It was a slaughter.

"We had a great day," said one soldier. "We killed a lot of people."

But the breakneck pace of the advance could not continue. Soldiers were beyond exhaustion, equipment was breaking down, and troops were in danger of outrunning their supply lines. Just north of Najaf and before going on to Karbala the ground war paused – although Iraqis on the receiving end might not have noticed. While the troops of ▶111

THE PRICE OF LIBERATION – A NEW DOOR

A bullet fired through the lock on his front door was how Fawaz Alavan found out the Americans had arrived in Baghdad. Until then he had believed the propaganda of Saddam Hussein's regime that the US forces were no closer than Najaf, 100 miles away to the south.

But as American troops conducted house-to-house searches to clear an enclave in the outskirts of the city, the chemical engineer learned they were literally on his doorstep. "I could not believe it," he said. "They were meant to be far away. Not outside my home."

The American advance into their city appears to have taken the people of Baghdad by surprise. Residents said they had believed the explosions which accompanied the attack were a continuation of the aerial bombardment. Even on seeing US armour, many had not realised.

Khalid, a taxi driver, described how he had presumed they were Iraqi.

"I was taking four women to Babylon," he said. "We thought it was just Saddam ordering soldiers south. Then we were stopped at a checkpoint and realised the Americans were here."

Throughout the day the Americans consolidated their position in the enclave. Two battalions of the 2nd Brigade were sent south to engage the remaining units of the Republican Guards' Medina division isolated by the speed of the advance.

The United States military believe that in the two days of fighting to secure its enclave in the south of Baghdad, the 2nd Brigade killed 700 Iraqi soldiers, destroyed around 300 vehicles, including 100 tanks, and took 60 prisoners of war.

At mid-morning the chemical weapon protection level was dropped to MOP One, the lowest of five levels of emergency, after it was assessed Saddam would not use chemical weapons within Baghdad. For soldiers who had worn the same anti-chemical suits since crossing the Kuwait border the news was a huge boost.

By mid-afternoon a trickle of American supply trucks had begun to arrive from bases south of the city of Karbala, bringing much needed ammunition, fuel and – most important for soldiers who had been baking in the 95F heat and high humidity – water.

At Mr Alavan's home, the forecourt had been adopted by one of the US battalions as a fuelling stop. He had ordered his sons to bring glasses of hot, sweet tea for the American soldiers. He then showed me the bullet holes in the metal and the smashed glass in the door panes. The side door had been kicked open by infantrymen.

"We were all very frightened," he said. "But the Americans come in and say, 'Sorry, sorry, sorry' about the damage. The Americans are good. When this war is over we will talk about Saddam, but now it is still too dangerous." Pausing for a moment's thought, he then added, "And when war is over I will also talk to the United Nations, Blair and Bush as they must pay for a new door."

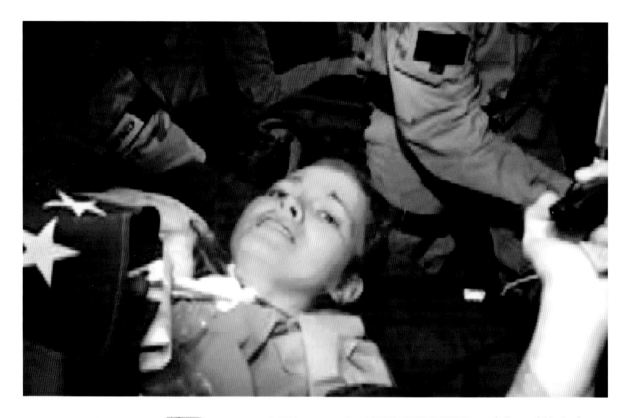

Rescued: Pte Jessica
Lynch is carried to
freedom on a stretcher
covered in the Stars and
Stripes after US troops
received a tip-off on her
whereabouts from an
Iraqi lawyer.
Her captured colleagues,
including Shoshana
Johnson, left, would
have to wait for another
two weeks before they
were liberated

DAY 12 31.03.03
Right: A British
Challenger tank crew find
time to relax as the sun
sets over Basra

Saddam's 'Victory' arch in Baghdad, a hollow tribute to the war with Iran he never won, stands wreathed in smoke as allied tanks, driving ever northward, continued to close in on the capital

DAY 13 01.04.03

Hungry children outside the southern village of Gul Ashab wait for food to be handed out by British troops.
Their anxious look is mirrored in the eyes of many Iraqis, caught amid the ravages of war, numbed by years of tyranny and worried by what liberation might mean for them

Next page: A vehicle commander with the Household Cavalry wipes dust from his eye

▶ 3rd Infantry Division rested, the air war continued its relentless pounding of targets across the country. Ahead of the 3rd Infantry were the dug-in troops of the Medina division. The ferocity of the bombardment they received cannot be imagined.

The war now took another unexpected turn. At a checkpoint near the city of Najaf, soldiers of the 3rd Infantry Division were on duty, searching the cars and trucks that crawled in and out of the city. It was tedious work, and the soldiers were edgy.

When another taxi approached, the men thought nothing of it as the driver beckoned them to come over. But as they stepped forward, the car exploded sending razor sharp shrapnel in all directions. When the smoke cleared, four of the soldiers lay dead.

A desperate weapon in the Iraqis' shrinking arsenal had been unleashed – the suicide bomber. In Baghdad, Iraqi Vice-President Taha Yassin Ramadan said the suicide bomber was an Iraqi soldier. Ramadan promised more attacks.

"To me this is not an act of war," said one US soldier. "It's terrorism."

The suicide bomber was praised as a hero on Iraqi state television. Saddam awarded him two posthumous medals.

Then, out of the blue, came good news for the allies. Hollywood could not have come up with a better plot when, on Saturday, March 29, a young Iraqi lawyer, Mohammed al-Rehaief, surrendered to US marines in Nasiriyah. He had the answer to the question troubling thousands of people across America: where was 19-year-old Private Jessica Lynch.

Some hours earlier al-Rehaief had been in the Nasiriyah hospital, visiting his wife, a nurse. According to an American newspaper, he saw a number of guards around a bed on which lay a young, obviously non-Arab, woman, bandaged and covered in a white blanket. He watched as a black-clad Fedayeen commander slapped her twice in the face.

"My heart cut," he said later. "There and then, I decided to go to the Americans to give them important information about the woman prisoner."

He set out on foot to walk the six miles to the nearest US checkpoint. After telling the marines his story, he was whisked away by Humvee to the battalion HQ, where he went over the detail again. Over the next 48 hours he acted as the eyes and ears of the US marines, revisiting the hospital to gather information. Where were the guards? How

many were there? Did they patrol? What weapons did they have? Where was Lynch in relation to the doors? Which bed was she in? Where was her room?

In all, the young lawyer drew five maps of the compound. Before midnight on Tuesday, the marines put their plan in motion. Marine Task Force Charlie, under the command of Major Mike Tanner, a Royal Marine Commando on attachment to the US marines, launched a diversionary attack elsewhere in

DAY 14 02.04.03

Above: An Iraqi soldier lies in the road next to his bombed-out vehicle

Below: US troops examine a briefing room abandoned by retreating Iraqi forces. One seat was said to be designated 'chemical adviser'

Nasiriyah to draw Iraqi militiamen away from the hospital. As that attack went in, other marines ferried US Navy Special Forces, the Seals, by helicopter to the hospital.

As the first Seal burst on to the ward he called out Lynch's name. There was no answer. Terrified by the gunfire, she had buried her head under the bedsheets. He called again: "Jessica Lynch, we're United States soldiers and we're here to protect you and take you home." She looked up at him, "I'm an American soldier, too," she replied.

An Army Ranger doctor examined her and prepared her for evacuation. The Seals strapped her to a stretcher, then carried her down the stairwell and into the waiting helicopter. A Special Forces cameraman filmed the operation which was broadcast around the world. Hours later a joyful Central Command spokesman told the press: "America doesn't leave its heroes behind. Never has. Never will."

The badly injured soldier, who had two broken legs and a broken arm, was flown to the US military hospital in Germany. There she received a hero's welcome.

Meanwhile in Basra, British troops were poised to move. For days they had encircled the city, allowing civilians to pass in and out but keeping pressure on the Iraqi ▶116

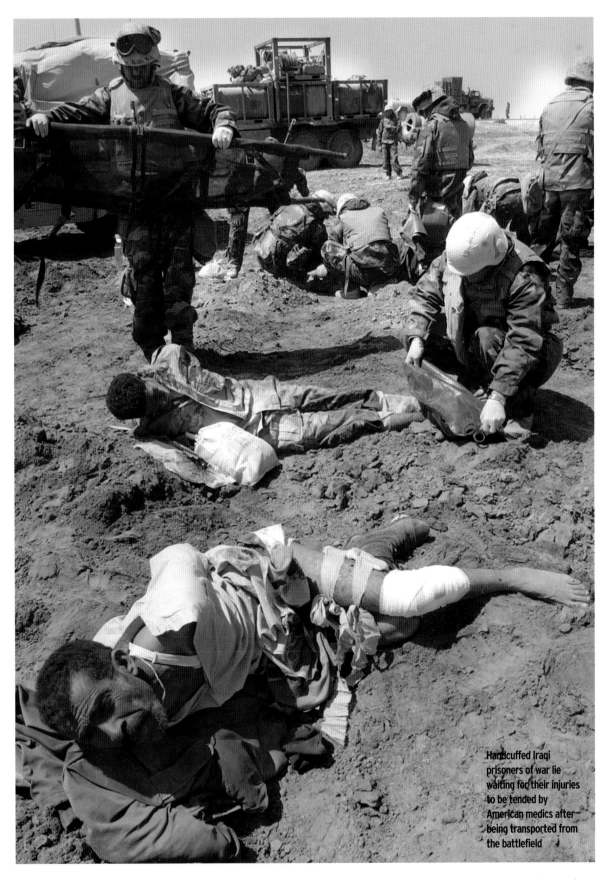

Handcuffed Iraqi prisoners of war lie waiting for their injuries to be tended by American medics after being transported from the battlefield

Commandos from the Queen's Dragoon Guards shelter from Iraqi rocket-propelled grenades outside Basra

17

▶ defenders with a series of raids, air strikes and aggressive patrolling.

All this time they were building up a detailed picture of life in Iraq's second city. Now Gen Brims decided the time was right to ratchet up the pressure. But rather than try to storm the city in one operation, he opted to take the city bit by bit, starting with the southern suburb of Abu al Khasib.

On April 1, hundreds of commandos from the Royal Marines launched the battle for Basra in a ferocious 15-hour assault on fortified Iraqi positions. The attack was the first all-out assault by a full commando since the Falklands conflict in 1982.

Under the codename Operation James, Alpha, Bravo and Delta rifle companies of 40

DAY 15 03.04.03
Above: An Irish Guardsman takes a tea break with a patriotic mug while patrolling on the outskirts of Basra

Commando, each of more than 120 men, advanced on foot at first light along a wide front trapping Iraqi forces up against the Shatt al Arab waterway.

They were backed by Challenger 2 tanks and Scimitar reconnaissance vehicles, while helicopters flew combat patrols and artillery fired barrage after barrage of support fire.

AS90 self-propelled howitzers were called in to deal with 21 Iraqi vehicles to the north of the Shatt al Arab, some believed to be T55 tanks. Allied drones had detected the build-up of armour and, after the AS90 barrage, they showed images of all 21 vehicles either badly damaged or destroyed.

As the soldiers from 40 Commando advanced, they were engaged time after time

Below: A woman injured in crossfire during a gun fight to secure a bridge over the Euphrates at Al Hindiyah sits next to the body of a man as a US officer calls in medical help

by enemy snipers and from bunker positions. At least one Dushka 12.7mm heavy machine gun was reported to have been used against the Marines before it was silenced.

Within an hour of Operation James starting, two senior Iraqi officers had been captured, four T55 tanks destroyed and at least one bunker blown up.

An additional company of men from 42 Commando were flown in by helicopter to help block an escape route for Iraqi troops.

Lt Col Gordon Messenger, the commanding officer of 40 Commando, reported that the 30,000 population of Abu al Khasib was "generally welcoming".

The British suffered one death in the attack. Marine Christopher Maddison, 9 Assault Squadron Royal Marines, aged 24, was killed when Iraqis in patrol boats staged a surprise attack on a landing craft patrolling the Basra canal, some 20 miles to the south.

That section of canal was believed to have been secured by Allied forces, but the Iraqis fired a rocket-propelled grenade at the craft, setting it on fire. Marines on shore fired at one of the Iraqi boats and sank it. The five crew members, three of whom were badly injured, were captured.

The operation went into a second day. Under cover from smoke shells fired by British gunners, troops from Delta Company of 40 Commando renewed the assault at first light, attacking two enemy positions, known by military planners (using the operation's James Bond theme) as Pussy and Galore. As two boatloads of Iraqi troops tried to flee over the Shatt al-Arab waterway they were attacked by mortars and helicopter-borne missiles.

By midday some sort of normality had returned to the riverside suburb and ▶120

Left: A spread-eagled corpse, killed in fighting to secure a bridge over the Euphrates, lies by the roadside

Below: Dust-coated marines are transported north after fighting in Nasiriyah

Right: Locals come out to watch a convoy of M1A1 tanks drive through their village after breaching the defensive ring around Baghdad

Below right: In the north, Kurdish peshmerga fighters are moved to the frontline in the battle for Mosul

▶ Royal Marine foot patrols began to seek out Saddam loyalists. They received a warm welcome from the 30,000-strong population.

Back in the north, after resting, the 3rd Infantry prepared to cross into the Red Zone. The division, which had been stretched out across a large swath of Iraq, regrouped in preparation for the attack on the Medina divi-

DAY 17 05.04.03
Above: One of the US Cobra helicopters, used to sweep the desert looking for enemy positions, prepares to take off after undergoing running roadside repairs

sion. Codenamed Peach, the operation was intended to secure the bridges over the Euphrates at Musayyib before Iraqi forces could destroy them. This was the last obstacle before Baghdad. But before they could get to it, they had to pass through the Karbala Gap, a narrow sandy plain between Lake Buhayrat and the Euphrates. US Military Intelligence

believed that crossing the Karbala Gap would trigger that most fearsome of battlefield weapons: nerve gas. Iraq's brutal Special Security Organisation had the sole authority to launch chemical attacks. It was believed they were alongside the Republican Guard. And everyone believed that they had their weapons with them.

Next page: American infantrymen from Charlie Company carry an injured comrade to a helicopter. He was shot in fighting as a US convoy drove through Baghdad

As the troops prepared to advance, orders came down that everyone had to be at a high level of chemical alert – suits on and done up, protective overboots donned, everything except the rubber gloves. Respirators were to be close at hand at all time.

Karbala lay some 70 miles to the north. It would not be a comfortable journey.

The burned-out shell of an Iraqi airliner lies on the tarmac at Saddam International Airport, scene of heavy fighting as coalition troops arrive in the outskirts of the capital

'A DAGGER IS POINTED AT THE HEART'

The coalition vice was tightening around Baghdad as the Desert Rats prepared to storm Basra. But where would Saddam's fearsome Republican Guard stage its last stand?

An Iraqi mother clings to her children as they cower in a ditch after being caught in crossfire during street fighting in Baghdad

The preparations for the move through the Karbala Gap had been unnerving enough. A surgical team had been assigned to the lead battalions to cope with casualties. Torn and damaged anti-chemical weapons suits had been replaced.

On the night of Wednesday, April 2, before the push started, the NCOs of 1st Battalion, 15 Infantry Regiment had been gathered to be addressed by Staff Sgt Trey Black. "This is going to be brutal," he told them. "Be prepared for what may be your last day on Earth."

As the order was given to move, Sgt Ray Simon rose out of his turret and shouted, "Come on you sons of bitches. I'm not scared of you. Bring it to me. I'm not scared."

In a series of rapid advances, the entire 3rd Infantry Division, now rested, re-grouped and re-armed, set off north. The 1st Brigade crossed the start line shortly after midnight. The 3rd Brigade set off a few hours later. Their task was to secure the gap for 2nd Brigade, to race through it and then to head for Baghdad.

Far in the distance, air strikes rocked Najaf's southern districts. One blast was so bright it momentarily turned night into day. Fires burned throughout the night.

By the time the 2nd Brigade prepared to roll, shortly after dawn, the news had filtered through that things were going better than expected. The crushing might of British and American airpower had done its job. The Medina division of the Republican Guard had simply ceased to function.

Supported by Apache helicopters, 1st Brigade had already seized a dam to the north of Najaf. Two Republican Guard T72 tanks, the most modern tank in the Iraqi arsenal, were in flames, their turrets blasted clear of the hull, and 82 prisoners, including two Iraqi colonels, had been taken.

Dawn broke on a beautiful day. Sunny and hot with barely a cloud, only the black smoke rising from destroyed targets in the distance interfering with the azure clear sky.

Throughout the day, the military radio kept up its constant crackle. The 1st Brigade had reached the Euphrates, crossing north of the city by midday, a destination it was not expected to reach before nightfall.

Units of 3rd Brigade were moving into the centre of the city from the east, catching the 14 Armoured Brigade of the Republican Guard Medina division, its weapons aimed towards the gap to their west, from the rear. There were still no reports of casualties.

DAY 18 06.04.03
An Iraqi soldier lies dead, his chest wounds covered by a plastic tray, as Irish Guardsmen come under fire during an advance into Basra

In the end, breaking through the Karbala Gap proved an anti-climax. At most, some 200 Iraqis mounted a series of running skirmishes, but the 3rd Infantry Division simply ploughed through them.

In a single day, the division had seized the bridge at Musayyib, north of Najaf, and the road to Baghdad lay open before them. The bridge had been wired with explosives, but the job had been botched, letting the army secure it intact. Working from boats, army engineers defused the explosives allowing two tank companies and one infantry company to roll across and suppress what little resistance remained on the far bank.

Clustered around their shortwave radios, which were tuned to the BBC, the troops learned that the marines were still pushing up in the east, putting into action the pincer movement they had been briefed about as they crossed the border from Kuwait.

The marines, having broken past Nasiriyah several days earlier, were advancing towards the central Iraqi town of Kut. Two divisions of the Republican Guard – the Baghdad and the al Nida – were believed to be standing in their way.

The destruction of Saddam's elite had begun on Tuesday with a feint. Regimental Combat Team 1 of the 1st Marine Division stormed up Highway 7 from the south, to persuade the Baghdad division that they were the main attack. The Iraqis took the bait with the Iraqi commander ordering his men to face the attack from the south. At this point the marines pulled their surprise.

Other teams circled back and moved on Kut from the west, hitting the Republican Guard in the flank. The speed of the pincer movement left the Iraqis reeling, with little chance to respond.

The Baghdad division had earlier been

American army medics carry the NBC reporter David Bloom to a medical unit near the Euphrates for treatment. The TV journalist later died from a thrombosis

brutally pounded from the air. US intelligence estimated that by the time the marines attacked it had barely half of its 11,000 troops and less than 25 per cent of its artillery left.

Overhead, AH1W Cobra helicopter gunships pounded Iraqi positions. The Americans ceased their onslaught for half an hour, using loudspeakers to offer the devastated division the chance to surrender. Their offer was ignored. The enemy was crushed.

But, as at Nasiriyah, the marines did not want to get sucked into street fighting. They simply detached a small unit to mop up Kut, while the rest swept on towards Baghdad.

Brig Gen Vince Brooks, the Centcom spokesman, told reporters in Doha, "The dagger is clearly pointed at the heart of the regime."

Throughout the next day the Americans drove the dagger deeper into the dying regime. As the advancing Americans ▶138

Airport arrival lounge: Soldiers with the 11 Engineering Battalion, Alpha Company, sit in a bullet-riddled hangar in the military section of Saddam International Airport after it had been secured by coalition troops

Down with Saddam: The people of Karbala celebrate on a toppled statue of Saddam Hussein, pulled down by Allied forces. Right, the Iraqi dictator bites the dust in Basra

DAY 19 07.04.03 British troops watch from their Challenger tank as young Iraqis carry off their haul

Royal Marines from Juliet Company 42 Commando line up outside Saddam's presidential palace in Basra

An Iraqi looter carries off an office chair, stolen from the Basra University campus

Members of the Republican Guard run along the bank of the Tigris, fleeing the onslaught as the allies take central Baghdad

DESPATCH
08.04.03 FROM TIM BUTCHER IN BASRA

PALACE EXPOSES DICTATOR'S GILDED TYRANNY

Dripping with dictator kitsch, Saddam Hussein's palace in Basra had everything a megalomaniac tyrant could wish for, from gold-plated lavatory brushes to French-made ornate lamp-posts entwined with climbing ivy.

There were Moorish screens carved from teak and giant marble-clad columns. There were vaulted ceilings and stained-glass windows. There was parquet flooring by the acre and sweeping staircases connecting ballroom to ballroom. A VHF radio system was fitted behind some of the panelling.

All was carefully arranged along the southern bank of the Shatt al Arab waterway, which had been channelled to form a deep, muddy-green moat spanned by graceful stone bridges.

"It really is an eye opener," Cpl Lee Waters, 28, from Portsmouth, said as he walked through one of the vast sets of double doors with other members of 42 Commando, Royal Marines, after the palace fell to advancing British troops. "This is what he spent his money on."

The Royal Marines had approached the palace gingerly, fearing booby traps, as they swept through the eastern suburbs of Basra to join up with troops from the "Desert Rats" – 7 Armoured Brigade – taking the centre of the city. But their caution appeared unfounded as the pink palace, made from a pale rose-coloured stone, was occupied only by a flock of doves.

Like so many of the presidential palaces built across Iraq in Saddam's regime, it was more a folly than a place of residence.

There had been no great effort to defend it. There were a few rusty bundles of barbed wire on the marble promenade but they had not been strung out for use. A cache of arms, found at the gate, lay unused and abandoned after the guards had fled. Sadly, it claimed one victim, when a British soldier accidentally shot himself in the foot with an AK47 as he prepared a pile of weapons for destruction.

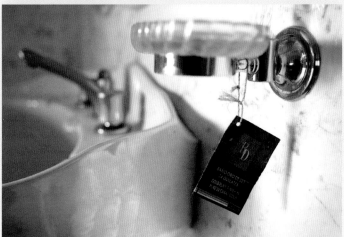

Like so much of Saddam's regime, the palace in Basra was designed to send a crude message to the Iraqi people: only one man in Iraq is powerful enough to afford such a palace and that man is Saddam Hussein.

Locals said it was less than six years old, built when Iraq was subject to strict trade sanctions and when Saddam's regime regularly claimed that its people were being starved by an American-led conspiracy.

Outside the opulent palace lay suburbs full of very poor people. Hundreds of them began to gather outside the gates after the Royal Marines had checked all the rooms for booby traps.

"There is gold in there," shouted one of the men. "Let us in, let us in."

For years these people had stared at the outside of Saddam's palace gates. Now they wanted to see with their own eyes what was on the other side.

Top: An infantryman from Charlie Company gives a Churchillian victory sign to comrades from the balcony of one of Saddam's Baghdad palaces.

Above: Gold-plated bathroom fittings, still bearing labels, give an indication of the opulent life enjoyed by the upper echelons of Saddam's regime

Right: A message is left in the dust of a banqueting table

▶ broke through the Republican Guard defences, they found the roads to the capital scarred with the debris of a defeated army. Burned-out tanks, struck from the air in attacks their crews could never have seen, littered the highways. Corpses lay under blankets. The ground was covered with discarded Iraqi uniforms, rifles and mortar ammunition. Abandoned gas masks, still sealed in their plastic bags, provided a reminder that a chemical attack might come at any time.

The toughest fighting the marines were to face in the east came in a clash with an Iraqi battalion of 30 tanks near Aziziyah, about 40 miles south-east of Baghdad. It was defeated.

Approaching the capital, marine commanders found a very different atmosphere among the people. In the south they had been treated at best with diffidence and at worst violent hatred. But as the marines travelled north along Highway 6, hundreds of Iraqi civilians came out on the streets to cheer the troops as they passed. At last the Iraqi people were greeting the coalition forces as liberators, not invaders.

One civilian, standing in the back of a pick-up as it drove past the marines, yelled out the only words in English that he knew, "George Bush!" Another man shouted, "You have saved us, you have saved us from him," while his weeping wife cried out, "I love you. I love you."

As the armoured jaws of the coalition's mighty vice closed slowly around the crumbling heart of Baghdad, Central Command unveiled video footage of a Special Forces raid into one of Saddam's palaces.

Maqar-el-Tharthar, the "Green Palace", on Lake Tharthar was the biggest and most elaborate of Saddam's many palaces. The compound covered two and a half square miles on the shore of an artificial lake in his home region, some 150 miles north of Baghdad. It had been completed in November 1993 and was Saddam's favourite place for fishing. The green-tinted video of the night-time raid was played during the Central Command news briefing in Qatar.

Army Delta Force and Air Force "Nightstalker" Special Forces blasted through the palace gates and dropped from helicopters into the grounds.

Glass shattered as the Special Forces teams, armed with stun grenades, night-vision goggles and silenced weapons, charged inside the opulent palace, racing from room to room. All was captured on camera by a reconnaissance plane and beamed back to commanders

The full monty: Members from 2 Platoon, 1 Parachute Regiment cool off in an improvised shower at their Basra base

in Qatar. Brig Gen Vincent Brooks admitted that the raid "did not yield any regime leaders" but said that it had uncovered key intelligence documents.

Centcom's reason for playing the video was to send a powerful message to Saddam and the Iraqi people – that coalition forces could operate anywhere and at any time they chose, and there was nothing the regime could do to stop them.

"It removes Saddam's aura of invincibility," said one official.

But this most extraordinary day of the war still had some surprises to spring. While the marines advanced up the eastern flank, the 3rd Infantry Division, meeting only light resistance, continued to push against the open door

of the feeble Iraqi defences. With seemingly unstoppable momentum, Gen Blount's division pressed on. Charging up roads running parallel to the four-lane motorway, the 2nd Brigade's next objective was a key junction, codenamed Saints, the meeting point of the main east-west and north-south highways. It fell into the brigade's hands without a struggle.

Meanwhile, the 3rd Brigade was ordered to advance north-west.

At around 7.30pm, Baghdad time, Task Force 3-69, the lead elements of the 3rd Brigade, saw through the stabilised night sights of their Abrams tanks the outer perimeter of their objective. Codenamed Lions, it was Baghdad's international airport, lying less than 10 miles from Saddam's palace on the

Next page:
Staff Sgt Chad Touchett, of A Company, 3rd Battalion, 7 Infantry, relaxes with a cigar in the marbled surroundings of a bomb-damaged Baghdad palace

Tigris. It was his only gateway to the rest of the world and it was now on the point of being slammed shut.

US Air Force F15E and F18 fighter jets were called in to strike the airbase with 2,000lb Jdam bombs. These exploded with thunderous claps as they struck barracks and hangars on the airport's northern side. Fighter-bombers from the USS Kitty Hawk targeted fuel and hangar facilities, also dropping 2,000lb bombs on a nearby military complex as the 1st Brigade unleashed its tanks and Bradley fighting vehicles. These smashed through the perimeter wall surrounding the 13,000ft runway and put down hundreds of rounds of suppressing fire. Iraqi defenders shot back with small arms and mortars, as well

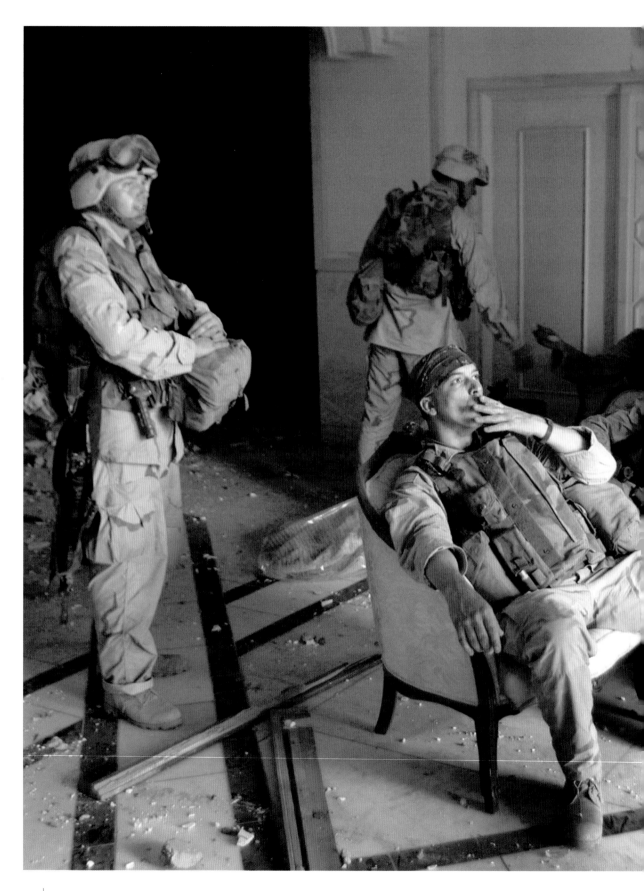

as the occasional artillery round. Battle raged through the night.

There was no respite for the defenders as the Americans, using their overwhelming night-time superiority, pressed home the attack.

As daylight broke over the airbase on Friday, April 4, the evidence of battle lay all around. Thousands of empty brass cases from the American M16 rifles littered the tarmac. Still the attacks carried on against the Iraqi defenders entrenched in the northern end of the airport.

An attempted counter-attack by Iraqi tanks was pulverised. By mid-morning the US commander told the press, "We own the airport." Later, Gen Brooks announced that the airport, formerly known as Saddam International Airport, had been renamed Baghdad International Airport. "It is a gateway to the future of Iraq," he said.

With US ground forces closing in on the capital it fell to the Iraqi Information Minister, Mohammed Said al-Sahaf, to explain away the disastrous setbacks the regime had suffered in the war. As he briefed reporters who had remained in Baghdad for the war, al-Sahaf didn't allow the facts to get in the way of a good story. His bombastic, melodramatic style had already earned him the epithet "Comical Ali" among the press. He was about to become an international figure of derision.

Calmly, he told the Baghdad news conference, even as the 3rd Division fought for control of the airport, that there were no American troops nearby. They were "not even [within] 100 miles" of the capital. They controlled no territory in Iraq, he said. "They are a snake moving in the desert."

Desperate to shore up the crumbling regime, the Iraqis turned to bizarre PR stunts. Unannounced, Iraqi state television suddenly started to broadcast some extraordinary footage. A blurred picture, which the station claimed was live, purported to show Saddam being mobbed while visiting bombsites in the capital. Several scenes contained images of people chanting, "Our blood, our souls we sacrifice to Saddam."

In the film of the walkabout, a smiling Saddam-like figure, wearing military uniform and flanked by a handful of aides, was seen holding up a baby and kissing it. In other shots he slapped hands with well-wishers and was even kissed by members of the crowd.

If the footage was of Saddam (and he was known to use several doubles), then it was the first time that he had been seen in ▶147

DAY 20 08.04.03
A soldier keeps a watchful
eye over members of the
Republican Guard who
were captured dressed in
civilian clothes. They are
being held behind razor
wire at an abandoned
military base outside Basra

DESPATCH

12.04.03 FROM OLIVER POOLE, WITH 3 BRIGADE COMBAT TEAM, BAGHDAD

THE HORROR OF BATTLE AND THE LONGING FOR HOME

It was dusk and a group of American soldiers were drinking coffee on the ramp of their combat vehicle in the rubble of what had once been part of a Baghdad housing estate.

One was softly singing: "Country roads, take me home, to the place I belong, West Virginia, mountain momma, take me home, country roads." The rest nodded agreement.

After months waiting in Kuwait and weeks of fighting in Iraq, the men who led the charge to Baghdad are close to returning to their bases in the United States. New units are meant to be on the way. The soldiers in Baghdad have been told they could be moved out within the next three weeks, and this has focused their minds.

Now that the threat of death has receded, the soldiers are beginning to dwell on what it took to secure their victory, and what awaits them when they get back to their families in America.

"Will they ever understand?" asked one of his wife and children in Georgia.

"Are you going to tell them what you have seen, what you have done?"

"Of course," answered the sergeant responsible for brewing the coffee, carefully pouring the hot water into paper cups. "There is nothing to be ashamed of. You did your duty. You won. Everyone will be proud."

"I don't know," said the first. "I don't know if I want them to know their daddy is a killer. That he saw dead bodies left in the road until they started to be eaten by stray dogs. I don't know if I even want to remember. Just leave it behind when we get the order out of here."

Some worry that it may be an experience they cannot put behind them.

"Will I be able to forget this, doc?" asked Specialist Woodward as he sat smoking a cigarette at the hatch of the medic van alongside his tank company's paramedic.

"Will I be able to walk down the street without ducking when a car backfires? Will life be normal again?"

There have been sights that will never fade. "It was a bunch of moments frozen," said Sgt Gerald Pyle, the tank commander who led the charge up the road from the Euphrates to Baghdad.

"I remember a man coming out of a car burning from his mid-thigh up. He got out as if going to get a hamburger and reached down to pick up an AK47 and we shot him. I remember a soldier looking up at me from his fox hole as I shot him. Snatches of time."

Some have found validation. In Kuwait, Pte Nitai Schwartz had complained the war was a mistake. By Baghdad, the 19-year-old had changed. "When I saw everyone waving I felt we had liberated them. Women were blowing kisses. For the first time in my life I felt like a hero."

In the entire 3rd Infantry Division, 60 Americans were killed. In the unit I was with, no one died, but 21 were injured.

All who saw combat know one unlucky bullet would have put them on that list and that knowledge haunts many of them. "It was when I saw that first person lying dead when we fought in Nasiriyah that I realised life is precious," said Sgt Norman Waver, 33.

"There was an Iraqi by the side of the road and I suddenly knew he, too, had a family, that having people who loved you would not stop anyone getting hit.

"I just want to go home now. Make sure my wife knows how much I love her. Show my kids the US. That is everything I suppose: the knowledge that life is precious, and not to waste it."

Right: The children of Basra show their contempt for Saddam Hussein by dancing on a portrait of the dictator which had been taken down in the city centre. It was later thrown in the river

Below: A weary US marine takes a rest during a patrol in the centre of Baghdad after the liberation of the Iraqi capital

DESPATCH

07.04.03 FROM MARTIN BENTHAM
WITH THE ROYAL SCOTS DRAGOON
GUARDS IN BASRA
AND NEIL TWEEDIE IN QATAR

DESERT RATS
STORM INTO BASRA

British forces stormed the centre of Basra yesterday, wresting control of large swaths of Iraq's second city from forces loyal to Saddam Hussein. Three British soldiers were killed in the action, along with many Iraqis.

The Ministry of Defence named one of the dead as Fusilier Kelan John Turrington, aged 18, of the Royal Regiment of Fusiliers. He was killed by a booby trap.

Challenger 2 tanks and Warrior fighting vehicles from battle groups of 7 Armoured Brigade, the "Desert Rats", mounted a three-pronged assault shortly after 5.30am local time. By dusk they had fought their way to the fringes of the Old City.

British officers in Qatar said 2,000 troops backed by 40 tanks had entered Basra in an operation which would continue through today.

The operation was ordered after Major Gen Robin Brimms, commander of 1st (UK) Armoured Division, decided the situation had reached "tip point", at which organised resistance was about to collapse.

Some Iraqis cheered and waved at the British while others turned on the Fedayeen paramilitaries defending the city. Several militiamen were killed by lynch mobs.

Furniture and other items were looted from government and paramilitary buildings as Shia slum dwellers on the outskirts of Basra flocked from their homes to capitalise on the British advance.

There was heavy fighting, with at least 120 Fedayeen reported killed by the Royal Scots Dragoon Guards battle group alone. Rocket-propelled grenades, Kalashnikov rifles and anti-tank missiles were all fired at the troops.

The assault on Basra was executed jointly by the Royal Scots Dragoon Guards battle group, the Black Watch battle group and the Royal Regiment of Fusiliers. Later, Royal Marines of 3 Commando Brigade advanced into the centre from the south, boxing diehard Iraqi forces into their stronghold, the district of Manawi Albasha.

The Royal Scots Dragoon Guards advanced along "Route Red" to destroy a factory compound occupied by militiamen and to secure a sprawling college in which large numbers of foreign paramilitaries including Syrians and Palestinians were hiding.

Within minutes the tanks were in action, firing into the factory complex and receiving rocket-propelled grenades in return. The complex was soon ablaze, killing many paramilitaries. When some fled, civilians from the nearby Shia Flats slum poured on to the streets in support of the British.

Some shouted and cheered, greeting the British soldiers with waves. Others took revenge on the men who for years had oppressed them, surrounding and attacking the fleeing Fedayeen.

A crowd descended upon one paramilitary, striking furiously at him and departed leaving him dead on the street. Gangs of looters appeared, seizing seemingly anything that was moveable from what remained of the Ba'ath Party buildings.

At the second principal target of the morning, a college of literature, the buildings appeared deserted.

But when a Challenger 2 commanded by Major Chris Brannigan crashed through the gates, dozens of Fedayeen suddenly emerged firing rocket-propelled grenades.

During the fighting some Fedayeen feigned death, before springing up in an attempt to fire grenades from close range.

Capt Niall Brennan of the Irish Guards pointed to the corpse of an assailant only a few yards away. "You see that dead guy. He's the guy that tried to kill me. A lot of them were playing dead, and he got up, brought his RPG to bear on me. I couldn't see him. The whole army net radio was screaming 'get down RPG 20 metres from you', but I had no idea where he was.

"One of my colleagues saw him and shot him. I would have known nothing about it if I hadn't been saved."

Later gunmen mounted a fresh attack on the British troops who had occupied the college area.

Clockwise from top:
Young girls cross the street after filling bottles in the daily water run in Basra

As the British take control of Basra , crowds of Iraqis flock across a pontoon bridge to the city centre. But the joy of liberation was soon to turn into a looting spree

A US marine from Fox Company removes anti-aircraft ammunition found in the Ba'ath Party HQ in Nasiriyah

Private Samantha Sheppard, of the 2nd Light Infantry Regiment, on patrol in Basra's back streets

▶ public for years. It was also to be the last.

In an act of unparalleled spectacle, the 3rd Infantry Division made their presence known to the Iraqi people on Saturday. Some 36 armoured vehicles, with 26 M1A1 Abrams tanks from 4-64 Armoured Regiment leading, made a 25-mile sweep through the southern suburbs and pushed west to the airport. The Americans were here and they wanted everyone to know it.

As the tanks roared through the streets, desperate Fedayeen fighters and members of Saddam's inner elite force, the Special Republican Guard, mounted suicidal attacks. The tanks at times ran a gauntlet of fire ▶150

A grateful Iraqi kisses
the hand of his liberator,
Capt Andy McClean of
Taskforce 2-69 Armour,
3 Brigade, on the road
into Baghdad

from RPGs, machine guns, and even 23mm and 57mm anti-aircraft cannons. The Americans replied with withering fire. Later, an American spokesman said that at least 1,000 Iraqis had been killed.

But live video footage of tanks on Baghdad's streets was not enough to convince "Comical Ali". He denied reports that American soldiers had reached the city centre, claiming Iraqi troops had defeated US forces at Baghdad's airport overnight. "Everything is okay," he said in another surreal performance.

Meanwhile in the south, the British commander, Gen Robin Brimms, decided to bring the suffering of the people of Basra to an end.

Above: The taking of the damaged Baghdad Highway Bridge. A US marine yells to comrades to charge as his unit advances under heavy fire

Days of aggressive patrolling by his troops had given the British land commander a clear idea of life in the city. He knew the city was his for the taking. He gave the order and took it.

Battle groups of 7 Armoured Brigade, the "Desert Rats", mounted a three-pronged assault shortly after 5.30am, local time, on Sunday April 6. There was a deafening roar as drivers of the Royal Tank Regiment started up the 12-cylinder, 1,200hp Perkins Caterpillar CV12 engines of their Challenger 2 tanks. In a cloud of dust, they departed into the darkness with Warrior fighting vehicles from the 1st Battalion Black Watch alongside them. Four miles ahead, lay the centre of Basra.

Along with the Black Watch battle group,

decks of the tanks and tried to prise open the hatches. According to one infantry officer travelling the Warriors behind, they had to "hose the tanks down" with machinegun fire.

One British soldier, Fusilier Kelan John Turrington, aged 18, of the Royal Regiment of Fusiliers, was killed by a booby trap.

By nightfall, most of the city was in British hands. There remained one redoubt for the diehard Iraqi forces, the district of Manawi Albasha, the heart of the old town. This was the last night that Basra would play unwelcome host to the oppressive regime.

Their day of liberation, Monday April 7, began inauspiciously as soldiers from the 3rd Parachute Battalion of 16 Air Assault Brigade gathered shortly after dawn at the city's College of Literature.

The complex, on the edge of the old city centre, had been seized the day before in bloody fighting that led to three British deaths. It was supposed to have been fully secured. But the sound of shooting, and news that at least two gunmen were sheltering inside the complex, delayed the paratroopers' departure while soldiers from the 1st Battalion Irish Guards dealt with the problem.

At about mid-day, the paratroopers, supported by tanks from the Royal Scots Dragoon Guards, began their advance. They moved out after being warned by their commanding officer, Lt Col John Lorimer, that they might well be confronted by "lunatics" who were prepared to fight to the death.

"You will need to use everything that you have learned in Northern Ireland and Pristina," he told his men.

The trepidation on the paratroopers' faces was clear as they began their walk into old Basra, splitting into two groups, taking parallel roads through the centre.

the Royal Scots Dragoon Guards and the Royal Regiment of Fusiliers were also heading into the city. Within minutes of crossing the start line, the lead tank of 2RTR's Egypt Squadron, belonging to the troop leader of 9 Troop, Lt David Pinkstone, quickly destroyed two bunkers and a T55 tank.

Elsewhere, the Royal Scots Dragoon Guards were in action, As the tanks rolled into the town, they were met with salvos of fire. The Soviet-era RPG7 bounced off the front of the Challenger 2. In desperation, the town's diehard fighters – mamny of them Arabs from Syria, the Lebanon and Egypt, tried to take out the tanks by feigning death. As the tanks rolled past, the attackers leapt on to the back

It was soon apparent, however, that their fears were groundless: a young boy walked up to the soldiers and flung a wad of Iraqi banknotes on to the ground and deliberately trampled on the face of Saddam displayed upon them.

As they passed through the "Gateway to Basra" crossroads which leads into the old city, looters pushing chairs, tables and other furniture passed by, seemingly oblivious to the British advance. One woman driver honked her car horn and waved as the paratroopers walked on, carefully scanning the horizon.

Soon the biggest problem was the swarm of children gathering around them, smiling and grasping at the hands of the paratroopers.

Within half an hour, the British forces were in the middle of the old district. Crumbling mud-brick buildings could be seen on either side of the road. The narrow warren of streets which comprise the Islamic Medina quarter stretched away to the right.

The only sign of potential Iraqi resistance was a group of sand-bagged trenches next to an anti-aircraft gun, alongside the Nadran River. But this, it turned out, had long been abandoned.

Below: An Iraqi soldier gives a comrade a lift on his motorcycle as they drive past a destroyed US tank in the southern suburbs of Basra

Right: Thumbs up from an Iraqi boy running alongside members of the Household Cavalry as they patrol Medina

Below right: The writing is on the wall as a soldier from 51 Squadron, the RAF Regiment, patrols Safwan

For the paratroopers, many of whom had feared for their lives at the outset, there was relief – and a sense of exultation – at the happy conclusion to the advance on Basra.

Pte Shahid Khan, 26, from Batley, West Yorkshire, said, "There were a couple of kids who came up to me and did high fives. It was a lovely gesture. I thought there was going to be a lot of resistance but now, it seems, it's going to be all right. The people have been brilliant. It's a very good day."

Further north, the decisive day for Baghdad and Saddam was about to dawn. The coalition was entering the endgame.

The fighting started even before the sun came up. With A10 Warthog tank-buster jets flying overhead, the 2nd Brigade of the 3rd Infantry Division rolled into central Baghdad, barrelling up on the south-western side of the Tigris with more than 70 tanks and 60 Bradley fighting vehicles. They met little resistance, sweeping past 200 anti-tank mines that had been spread on the road before them and heading for the presidential compound. They were fired on from a clock tower overlooking the complex but destroyed it with tank fire.

As he pushed on into central Baghdad, one officer with the US 3rd Infantry Division shouted out, "Saddam Hussein says he owns Baghdad. We own Baghdad."

By daybreak the Americans had parked their tanks on Saddam's lawns. It was then, that "Comical Ali", called his most bizarre press conference. From the roof of the Palestine Hotel, where western journalists were staying, he said over the noise of battle, "I reassure you Baghdad is safe. There is no presence of the American columns in the city of Baghdad. None at all."

Even as he was spoke, marines in the south-east of the capital were advancing strongly. Iraqi defenders fought running skirmishes but to no avail. By 10am, the marines were flooding into the centre, after securing bridges over the Tigris. As the American juggernaut rolled in, Iraqis were seen fleeing along the banks of the river. Some even jumped in.

Lt Col Pete Bayer, operations officer in the 3rd Infantry Division, said, "We have seized the main presidential palace in downtown Baghdad. There are two palaces down there, and we are in both of them."

The Republican Palace, the newest and grandest of Saddam's homes, still smoking from the blasts of cruise missile strikes, was stormed.

With Bradleys and Abrams outside, soldiers from the 3rd Battalion, 7 Infantry, moved into the bombed-out buildings. All around them was the evidence of Saddam's ostentatious lifestyle. A layer of thick dust covered the imitation French baroque furniture. Rooms were full of the shattered remains of gilt dining services and crystal chandeliers.

Initially, the coalition plan had been for the thrust to be another thunder run, a dramatic gesture of defiance and then withdrawal. But as night started to fall on the city it was clear the Americans were there to stay. They were in Baghdad, and they were not leaving it.

That night, as a postscript to one of the best days of the war, news came through that many in Iraq wanted to hear. Earlier in the week British forces had struck at the home of the infamous "Chemical Ali", General Ali Hassan al-Majid, a cousin and arch henchman of Saddam, and architect of the 1988 genocidal Anfal campaign against the Iraqi Kurds, which resulted in the murder and "disappearance" of some 100,000 Kurds.

After the raid, British officials admitted they had killed two of his bodyguards. It was not until later that they announced the raid had been a complete success. "Chemical Ali" was dead.

The night had one more surprise. A snatched conversation late on Monday appeared to be what the allies had been waiting for since the first failed attempt to assassinate Saddam at the start of the war,

Since that first attack, the encrypted radio system used by Saddam's lieutenants to contact other members of the Iraqi leadership had been silent, encouraging the hope that the Iraqi dictator was dead.

Any disappointment that had followed its return to the air waves was replaced with excitement at the apparent emergence of another opportunity to decapitate the Iraqi regime. Not only was the conversation being picked up by signals intelligence operators, it was being confirmed by sources on the ground. The Iraqi leader and at least one of his two sons, Uday and Qusay, were meeting with a number of the dictator's key lieutenants in a favourite restaurant frequented by senior Ba'ath Party leaders and military officers who lived in the Mansur area of Baghdad.

Within half an hour of the intelligence coming into CIA headquarters at Langley, Virginia, the co-ordinates of the restaurant had been flashed to allied air controllers.

The Awacs aircraft controlling coalition air movements over Baghdad had a B1 Lancer bomber already in the air, with four 2,000lb satellite-guided bombs on board 12 minutes from the target.

The US bomber had just taken on fuel from a tanker aircraft and was bound for pre-planned targets when it got the emergency order to divert to a new target.

§The bomber's crew were not told who they were going to attack but an air traffic controller in the nearby Awacs did give them a clue. "This is the big one," he said.

Flying at just under 30,000ft, the B1 dropped two GBU31 bunker-buster bombs, designed to penetrate deep into the target before they exploded, and, three seconds later, another two, this time with with 25-milli-second delayed fuses. All that was left of the target was a crater more than 50 yards wide.

Unfortunately for the Americans, the bombs missed. They did not strike the restaurant, but hit nearby homes, killing eight people, including three children. According to eyewitnesses, Saddam and his sons were not even in the restaurant.

But Saddam had no time to gloat. His tyrannical rule was at an end. Amid wild scenes of jubilation on Wednesday, April, 9,

only 17 days before his 66th birthday, his regime collapsed.

Journalists in the Palestine Hotel woke that morning to find their ever-present minders gone. The hotel had for days been the last bastion of the regime. Countless uniformed of Ba'ath Party officials had mingled with western journalists there. Suddenly that morning, there were none.

For a few hours the city was stuck in limbo. Then the US tanks rolled unmolested into the centre and the jubilant Iraqis gave them a tumultuous welcome.

Unshackled from the fear of 24 years' of oppression, the people turned on the symbols of the regime, tearing down statues and defacing pictures of the dictator, pelting them with rocks and smashing them to pieces.

Some chanted the praises of President Bush, while others took the opportunity to loot government buildings and shops. Many were openly thankful for their new-found freedom, standing in groups waving and shouting "America" and "Kill Saddam" as the US vehicles rolled past.

"It is a great feeling. I have never felt this way before," said Ayass Mohammed, a 20-year-old student. "It was only two hours ago when suddenly I feel freedom, when I saw the American tanks and heard that the regime had run. All my life all I know is Saddam. Now we are free."

By the afternoon, US tanks had reached al-Fardus Square, beside the Palestine Hotel. Here an ecstatic group of men turned on the statue of Saddam that stood on a marble plinth dominating the square. Hoisting themselves on to the statue's feet, they set about it with hammers and stones.

Then they tied a rope to its neck and tried

to pull it down. When they failed to topple the edifice, American soldiers placed a chain around its neck and attached it to a tank recovery vehicle. Cheers rose as the armoured vehicle's engine revved. Slowly the statue was torn down from its cement pedestal, crashing to the ground.

Within seconds, Iraqis swarmed all over it. Tearful men pounded the face with shoes and slippers – a grave insult in the Arab world. Others battered its face with sledgehammers. "I'm 49, but I never lived a single day. Only now will I start living," said Yussuf Abed Kazim, a local imam. With the statue lying on the ground, US Marines and Iraqis shook hands and hugged one another.

However, not all Baghdadis were happy at the Americans' arrival. Some stood with arms crossed, their faces grim. "How would you feel if there were foreign tanks outside your home?" asked Ahmed Kadra, 50.

"The young people they don't know life. They just think it is a revolution and we can dance and be excited. They do not have a relation to the land, our country. That is what we die for. That is all that matters." He stamped his foot on the pavement. "The land, that is ours, and others are trying to take from us."

In Baghdad, Saddam's regime went out with a whimper. If there was to be a last stand,

DAY 22 10.04.03

Above: The world watches as the statue of Saddam in central Baghdad is toppled, the symbolic end of his regime

Below: Iraqis stand on the damaged head of the fallen statue

Tikrit, his hometown, was the most likely setting. It lay 90 miles to the north.

As it had fallen to Sir Jeremy Greenstock, the British Ambassador to the UN in New York, to bring down the curtain on peace, so it now fell to the Iraqi Ambassador to the UN to bring down the curtain on Saddam's regime.

Mohammed Al-Douri, getting into a car outside his residence in New York, turned to the press, straightened himself and said the final words of Saddam's regime. "The game is over. We hope the peace will prevail. That's all." With that he turned and drove away.

Council of war: Members of the Royal Scots Dragoon Guards prepare battle plans in a basement outside Basra. Officers were trying to judge the strength of the enemy presence in the city

A US marine commander sits in his armoured vehicle amid a traffic jam on the road into the newly-liberated city of Baghdad

'THIS IS AN EX-REGIME'

The fall of Baghdad triggered an orgy of looting as liberated Iraqis ransacked the citadels of the fallen regime. Now coalition troops were marching on Saddam's last stonghold, his home town of Tikrit . . .

It was the forgotten front. While the American troops poured into the south of Iraq, the northern half of the country remained firmly in Iraqi hands. But it was only a matter of time. In the most northern reaches of the country lay the semi-autonomous region of Kurdistan. Although still a part of Iraq, Saddam's writ did not reach this far. The region achieved a state of tense freedom after the 1991 Gulf war, when the coalition sent in troops through Turkey to protect the safe enclaves.

The Kurds had every reason to despise

Above: An American soldier chooses some postcards to send home as shops reopen in Baghdad

Below: The leaders of the pack. Saddam Hussein and his son Uday feature on the Pentagon's deck of most-wanted members of the Iraqi regime

Saddam. On April 16, 1987, the Iraqi dictator opened a new chapter in infamy when he became the first leader in history to use chemical weapons against his own people. Kurdish Balisan was a sizeable village, which was home to about 1,750 people. It had four mosques, a primary school and an intermediate school.

In the drizzly late afternoon of April 16, the villagers were preparing dinner when the sound of a dozen approaching aircraft was heard, followed by muffled explosions.

A cool evening breeze was blowing off the mountains, and it brought strange smells – suggestive of roses. "But then," reported one elderly woman, "it was all dark, covered with darkness. We could not see anything, and were not able to see each other. It was like fog. Then everyone became blind." Some vomited. Faces turned black; people experienced painful swellings under the arms, and women under their breasts. Later, a yellow watery discharge oozed from their eyes and noses. Many who survived suffered problems with their sight, or total blindness, for up to a month. In Sheikh Wasan, a woman was seen staggering around blindly clutching her child, not realizing it was dead.

According to one report, at least 225, and

DAY 23 11.04.03:
A US Bradley armoured vehicle drives under the arm of the huge arch of swords at Saddam's military parade ground in Baghdad

Top: Looters carry away wooden furniture as they pass a burning house in central Baghdad

Above: A rest after their labours for young Iraqis as they lounge in a cartload of stolen chairs

Left: An ornate chair is carried from a presidential palace

possibly as many as 400, died that day. Revenge for this and other attacks was to come 16 years later, almost to the day.

Watching events unfold to the south, the Kurdish fighters, or peshmerga, working closely with US Special Forces, waited. Intense diplomatic pressure from Turkey, with its long troubled history with the Kurds, was applied to stop the Kurds swooping down and seizing the oil-rich cities of Kirkuk and Mosul. America promised to act as the restraining influence.

The original allied invasion plan envisaged the US 4th Infantry Division passing through Turkey to attack Baghdad from the north. Ankara, however, blocked the move. Instead it fell to the Kurds to act as a proxy army for Gen Franks.

From the first stages of the war, Iraqi positions in the north were subjected to intense US air strikes. Hundreds of high-precision, satellite-guided bombs smashed into tanks, artillery and infantry positions in the northern cities.

As the allied encirclement of Baghdad progressed, Iraqi troops began to pull out of their front-line positions in the north, retreating to the cities that they hoped would offer more protection. The watching peshmerga advanced into the vacuum. Still the Americans acted as a brake.

But when on Wednesday, April 9, the statue of Saddam was symbolically brought to its knees before the people of Baghdad, it was clear that no one could stop the jubilant Kurds. History was now on their side.

The next day, they poured into Iraq's northern oil capital, Kirkuk, in their thousands. They arrived shooting in the air and whooping with joy, as the people of Kirkuk came out on to the streets chanting, singing and dancing deliriously. Others turned on the symbols of Baghdad's collapsing regime, tearing down posters and portraits of Saddam and looting government stores.

Relatives separated for months or years by Saddam's security police were reunited in emotional scenes. Refugees, forced out of their homes years before, rolled into town in battered orange and white taxis to reclaim what was theirs.

The servants of Saddam's regime, having suffered weeks of American air strikes, simply packed up and left. Witnesses said they saw them in long, sprawling convoys on the road to Tikrit, the powerbase of Saddam's clan.

Many of the Kurdish fighter who liberated Kirkuk were from the city but had ▶166

DESPATCH
09.04.03 FROM JACK FAIRWEATHER IN BASRA

SADDAM HAS NOT DESTROYED MY HOPE

At dawn yesterday Haider went for a stroll past his girlfriend's house in central Basra, as any eager lover might.

But for Haider, a member of Iraq's small pro-democracy movement, it was the first time he had openly left his house in 12 years. He had not seen his fiancee in six years.

"Saddam has taken away everything I have, except one thing," said Haider, a small man, who looked frail despite being only 28 years old. "He has not destroyed my hope for democracy and freedom."

Haider's fight against the regime began after his father, a leading lawyer in Basra who also worked in the Foreign Ministry, was arrested by Saddam's secret police in 1991 for trying to contact the Iraqi opposition in exile. He has not seen him since.

"That was during the first Gulf war, when I last felt hope that we might be liberated," said Haider, in English gleaned from hours of listening to American radio stations.

Within days Haider and his family were placed under house arrest. "I was removed from medical college, our house was taken away and we were forced to live on the little money my sister could send us from Jordan," he said.

"I began trying to contact some of my father's friends. It seemed important to carry on his work."

In 1997 he met his future fiancee. "We were to be married, but the secret police found out before our wedding and forced her family to intervene unless I told them everything I knew.

"I refused, because how could I give in to them? I'd rather sacrifice anything, just anything, rather than democracy. I then spent a year in Iraqi jails where they beat and tortured me, but I would not tell them what they wanted.

"I left prison very ill, but I had a little medical knowledge from my studies to help me get better and was able to continue my resistance."

From an inner pocket of his jogging trousers Haider took a list of numbers of contacts in America. "I always knew the Americans and British would come and rescue us. During the siege I told people not to worry, that you would be here soon.

"It is the little details of freedom which have sustained me." He removed from his wallet a hymn sheet for the British national anthem and, in unsteady handwriting, the words "Challenger and Warrior tanks".

Haider, who had so far been speaking in an American accent, suddenly shifted to a strange form of Cockney. "See," he said proudly, "I have also been listening to the BBC World Service."

He also carried a cheap sketchbook containing drawings in ballpoint pen of deserted beaches, of birds caught in motion over cliffs and of swimming dolphins.

"They are all from my own mind," he said. "They are my little pictures of freedom.

"But now there are some things I have to do. I must make myself well and see my beloved before I return to work, helping the people of Iraq enjoy democracy."

DAY 24 12.04.03
Iraqi banknotes
bearing the face of
Saddam Hussein lie
torn and burnt in
the street after
looters ransacked
a Baghdad bank

been brought up in refugee camps in the Kurdish autonomous region to the east and north after their parents were expelled by Saddam's secret police.

"I feel like I am reborn," said Abdullah Najib.

The next day, Thursday, April 10, Kurds and US Special Forces walked into Mosul after the Iraqi garrison surrendered en masse.

That left the only one important town outside the allies' control – Tikrit, Saddam's home and the spiritual heartland of the Ba'athist regime.

A convoy of US marines, backed by tanks, AH1W Super Cobra attack helicopters and

prise on the road north. Filmed live on American TV, allied troops rescued the last remaining US prisoners of war.

The six men and one woman were found 40 miles north of Baghdad after an Iraqi policeman approached the marines and told them where the PoWs were.

The troops holding the seven had released them after being deserted by their officers. Five of the PoWs were members of the 507th Maintenance Company who had been captured with Pte Jessica Lynch in the ambush near Nasariyah in which seven of their comrades had been killed. The remaining two prisoners were the crew of an Apache attack helicopter. These were the last US servicemen unaccounted for.

The last stand of the Republican Guard in the stronghold of their feared leader proved to be the final anti-climax of the campaign. The Adnan division, entrusted with the defence of Tikrit, had simply evaporated.

Abandoned Iraqi tanks littered the outskirts of the town, although there were some skirmishes in which a number of Iraqis died. Five tanks were destroyed, but resistance amounted to little more than several pockets of diehard paramilitaries.

After just 26 days, American marines had taken possession of Saddam's palace in Tikrit. "The Iraqi army has been destroyed. There's no regime command and control in existence right now," said Gen Franks. "This is an ex-regime."

Back in the major cities, decades of repression was unleashed in a maelstrom of violence. It began against the symbols of the regime, but degenerated into indiscriminate looting.

Like a Biblical plague it spread through liberated Iraq, starting in Basra. Baghdad was stripped almost bare.

Joyous looters took away anything they could carry. Children passed with neon lights. Shi'ite women, cloaked in black veils, piled furniture, chairs, even air-conditioning units on to wheelbarrows. Men carried away computer screens, giving the thumbs-up sign to photographers.

One reporter saw a man leading away a magnificent thoroughbred by the bridle. "He comes from the personal stable of Uday, Saddam's son," he explained. A Ford Mustang full of cases of whisky passed by, a young man sitting on the boxes in the open boot.

More alarmingly, hospitals were ransacked, drugs stolen and incubators wheeled out into the streets. Doctors working in the

FA18 Hornet jets, moved on the city from Baghdad. As they advanced north they encountered what were clearly the remnants of a broken army, a line of unarmed men drifting back to the capital. But the marines remained cautious. There were reports that up 2,500 diehard loyalists were still in the city, prepared to fight to the death. Crushing Saddam's last stronghold could still be a bloody business.

Minders accompanying a CNN camera crew, including Brent Sadler, were forced to shoot their way out of Tikrit after trying to film there.

There was one more morale-boosting sur-

KISSES GREET THE LIBERATORS OF KIRKUK

If there was ever a case of gratitude too great for words to express it was in the eyes of the men, women and children of Kirkuk's Stall Street yesterday.

First they clapped wildly, then they shouted, then they kissed our grimy cheeks with passion. Goran, a 15-year-old wearing a sweatshirt with St Audrey's Convent School emblazoned on it, sat on the floor, knees touching mine, and beamed.

"America, America, Bush, Bush," he chanted repeatedly. His cousin Zainab, a 15-month-old girl with paralysed legs, a result of cerebral palsy, smiled, infected by the joy.

Fadil Talib, a 45-year-old agricultural manager, said with tears in his eyes: "No more killings, chemical attacks and disappearances. At last I can live a normal life." The liberation of Kirkuk yesterday unleashed scenes of joy not seen in this demoralised, unlovely city for decades.

The day had started on the other side of the front line, where the Kurdish peshmerga guerrillas had been preparing to march on Kirkuk, a city they consider their spiritual capital, for weeks.

Each had been issued with ammunition and assigned a point from which to enter the besieged city but they had been told to wait until the order to advance came from Washington and London.

The previous night we had heard rumours that Kirkuk might be ripe for falling and had risen before dawn. A two-hour journey on a stony smugglers' track took us to a village barely six miles to the north of the city, which had been under heavy Iraqi fire only three days

before. By late morning, hundreds of peshmerga had gathered and were milling around impatiently.

Bais, a 76-year-old grandfather of 12, was carrying a Russian Draganov sniper rifle. He said, "I am so impatient I'm on fire."

Then the word came: the Iraqis had fled Kirkuk's Kurdish suburbs. No clearer order was needed. Motorbikes revved, men shouted orders and the first pick-ups began to roll. We followed.

The road across the front line was strewn with rubble. There was a huge oil stain, a large earth barricade and a smashed concrete building with a fading picture of Saddam Hussein painted on it.

Then, on the left, a long line of Iraqi prisoners of war walked past, their heads bowed. Behind them, the ridge they had held until so recently was abandoned, smoke still billowing from one of their bunkers.

"It's finished," a Kurdish man screamed at the top of his lungs.

Adnan, my driver, flushed with excitement. A former policeman from Kirkuk, he had been thrown out of the force 15 years ago because he was a Kurd. Three weeks ago he had fled a Mukhabarat secret police round-up in Kirkuk, leaving his wife and children behind.

For days, as we worked the front

Cheers as the Kurdish flag flies over Kirkuk

lines, I had caught him gazing worriedly at the smoke clouds over his native city. Now as we surmounted the last hill, he grinned broadly, kissed his fingers and touched his forehead with them.

Less than five minutes later we were in the city – the first westerners to enter in weeks, perhaps months. At the sight of our faces, the Kurds in the street simply broke down with joy. A middle-aged man held my neck and refused to let go for several seconds. He cried like a baby.

We headed deeper into town towards the Arab sector. Here the mood was more menacing. Shooting broke out and more than once we were forced to run for cover.

At Tabakchaly Bridge, the main road to the east, a middle-aged man lay dead by the roadside. There was a rumour he was a secret policeman, though nobody was sure.

Opposite was the Ba'ath Party's telephone bugging centre, but the equipment had been shipped out before the regime fled. Here the mood was more restrained, shutters bolted and fewer people on the streets. As we watched, two groups of looters drew guns on each other.

Further to the south of the city, there was still fighting. Near the old Ba'ath Party headquarters, shattered by a US bomb, several peshmerga were attempting to root out hardline Saddam loyalists.

For half an hour we watched as rounds were exchanged and mortars, apparently fired by the Iraqis, fell among the spacious villas. Then the peshmerga moved in for the kill. Minutes later a Fedayeen officer lay dead by the roadside, blood on his shirt and wallet.

They beat another, turning his face into a bloody pulp. The peshmerga turned to us: "Shall we kill him? Shall we kill him? He killed one of our men."

As darkness fell last night, gunfire was still echoing around the city. But there were also the sound of car horns and jubilant singing.

buildings had to arm themselves to keep the looters at bay.

Iraq's National Museum was ransacked, occasioning international outrage. In one of its rooms, 26 statues of Assyrian kings, all dating back at least 2,000 years, were decapitated.

The pillaging, part of a general collapse in law and order in the capital, represented the senseless destruction of Iraq's national memory. When the Mongols conquered Baghdad in 1258, they sacked the city and destroyed its library. This time, Iraqis chose to ransack their own capital and with it the legacy of their own past.

Slowly, however, the destructive frenzy subsided as a nervous peace returned.

At this point, the Americans, in a theatrical flourish, released a list of the most wanted Iraqis – in the form of playing cards. Saddam was the ace of spades; his sons Uday, the ace of hearts, and Qusay, the ace of clubs.

So rounding up the former Ba'athist henchman became an international game of rummy. First to be captured was Amir Hammoudi al-Sa'adi, senior scientific adviser, liaison to the UN weapons inspectors and the public face of Saddam's programme of obfuscation to hide evidence of his illegal weapons

Three of the American prisoners of war, missing since the opening of the war and now abandoned by their captors, are taken away for a medical check-up. Advancing marines were told of their whereabouts by an Iraqi policeman

programme. And as the days went on other figures fell into American hands.

Of these, the most recognisable to the West was Tariq Aziz, Saddam's former deputy prime minister (8 spades). But also taken were Muzahim Sa'ab Hassan al-Tikriti, the Iraqi air defence commander (Queen of diamonds), Barzan al-Tikriti, Saddam's half-brother and ex-head of the Iraqi Intelligence Service (5 clubs), and Gen Zuhair Talib Abd al-Sattar al-Naqib, the former head of Military Intelligence (7 hearts).

With the military campaign now complete, the far more difficult task of winning the peace had to begin. The sudden collapse of the Ba'athist regime left a vacuum at the heart of Iraq. Whoever stepped into that void would be well placed to shape Iraq's reconstruction. Accordingly, numerous factions began to claim their stake.

For decades, Saddam's security apparatus had suppressed the majority Shias, but with the fall of the regime, they were quick to reassert themselves.

Schism broke out in the holy city of Najaf. The moderate cleric Abdul Majid al-Khoei, was hacked to death outside the Shrine of Ali, one of the most sacred Shia sites, by a mob

armed with swords. He had flown out to the city from exile in Britain only days earlier to help in Iraq's reconstruction of the country. Now other clerics began to assert their claim to be the spiritual leader of the Shia.

For America, the establishment of a fundamentalist theocracy would be disastrous. To avoid this and to oversee reconstruction, they were quick to fly in their own civil administrator, the former US general Jay Garner, who had played a key role in setting up the Kurds' autonomous enclaves after the 1991 Gulf war.

One of his first acts was to convene meetings in Baghdad of 250 prominent Iraqis, including members of the Shia community, to help form an interim administration – though controversy surrounded the Pentagon's favoured candidate to run this interim regime. Ahmad Chalabi, leader of the Iraqi National Congress, is a former banker with a chequered past, who has failed to win the confidence of many in the Bush administration.

By mid-May, as even a mobile phone network failed to appear in Baghdad, Garner had been replaced by the diplomat and hawkish conservative, L Paul Bremer III. The White House had concluded that, to win international confidence and the trust of the Iraqi people, a civilian face was needed at the helm. At the same time, spiritual leader Mohammed Baqer al Hakim, head of the Supreme Council of Islamic Revolution in Iraq, returned after 23 years in Iran, and was expected to play a central role in building a new administration.

Internationally, the fallout from the Iraqi war could continue for years, possibly decades. The diplomatic knuckle fights that plagued the run-up to hostilities put a huge strain on western alliances – in Nato, the European Union, and the United Nations. Relations between Paris and Washington were near breaking point and America's links with Russia and Germany came under intense pressure.

Tony Blair also paid a price. His relations with Paris, Berlin and Moscow were damaged and the decision to go to war cost him a Cabinet minister, Robin Cook.

On Friday, May 2, President Bush stood on board the USS Abraham Lincoln and told the world the war was over. The fact that neither Saddam nor his sons had been accounted for, that no evidence of weapons of mass destruction had been uncovered, that no firm link had been established between Iraq and al-Qa'eda and that no concrete plans for the country's future existed did not deter the 43rd president from declaring victory. ■

Iraqi women, dressed in traditional chador, are frisked by a female American soldier at a Basra checkpoint

FALL OF TIKRIT
ENDS THE WAR

Saddam Hussein's home town fell to American troops yesterday, ending the last major military operation of the war in Iraq.

As marines, backed by tanks and helicopters, captured the centre of Tikrit, the spiritual homeland of the Ba'athist regime, senior officers signalled that the 26-day campaign was nearly over.

Brig-Gen Vincent Brooks, speaking at the coalition headquarters in Qatar, said that what he termed decisive military operations were "coming to a close".

The Pentagon announced that two of the five aircraft carriers close to Iraq were being recalled. The Kitty Hawk and Constellation could soon be followed by a third.

At the same time, America stepped up attacks on Syria, saying that it faced economic sanctions if it did not reform and accusing it of testing chemical weapons.

Donald Rumsfeld, the US defence secretary, said, "I'd say that we have seen chemical weapons tests in Syria over the past 12-15 months."

Tony Blair claimed victory in Iraq for the first time and told the Commons that he hoped elections could be held there in little over a year. While there was no mood of "triumphalism" among the British and American forces, "the cause was just, the victory right", he said.

Brig-Gen Tim Cross, the senior British official involved in the American effort to run Iraq since the fall of Saddam, said he hoped an administration would be set up in Baghdad in two weeks and that oil sales would be held in three months.

It had been feared that Saddam's Tikrit heartland might prove the scene of a desperate last stand, but in the end there was little resistance.

There were cautious if genuine waves from people who emerged from alleys on to the main street, where each lamp-post bore a portrait of Saddam. Unlike in Baghdad, they and the statues were intact.

Cars with white cloths tied to wing mirrors made brief, wary explorations before disappearing. Near the main American checkpoint a single tea shop opened in a line of otherwise closed shops.

Among the huddles of people who came on to the streets, none said they had ever seen Saddam. Every year lavish birthday celebrations had been held. Children sang songs of tribute to Saddam,

parades lauded his glorious record and dignitaries handed the governor gifts for the "Great Uncle".

But Tikritis said they guessed Saddam was visiting only when the telephones and power were cut for a few hours and convoys of black cars with tinted windows slid into town.

Late last week, the poorer residents who stayed behind saw plenty of smart cars heading out of the city. They belonged to Saddam's local henchmen, senior Ba'ath Party members, civil servants and military leaders. Tikritis assume they have taken refuge in the many mud-brick villages and hamlets in the vicinity.

As in other towns captured by the allies, the inhabitants demanded restoration of law, order, electricity and water. "We accept the Americans here but we need stability," one man said. "We have been bombed for three weeks; no water for three weeks. We want to work again."

The Americans entered the small city cautiously, with at least four gunships flying low over armoured fighting vehicles. As they rolled through the gates of the university campus just after noon, a helicopter unleashed several missiles on a building on the edge of the compound where suspected loyalists were believed to be holed up.

Tikrit, which contains several of Saddam's lavish palaces, was rocked by blasts throughout the day as units continued "clearing" operations. As night fell, marines put barbed wire around the city centre and heavy bombing continued as aircraft hit targets on the outskirts.

Now that the Iraqi army has been routed, US efforts are switching to the hunt for Sadda.

As the marines pushed rapidly north towards Tikrit, they made a short detour to the village of al-Ouja, where Saddam was born.

Brig Gen John Kelly said, "We were looking for evidence that he had been buried but there was nothing. The village was abandoned."

DAY 26 14.04.03 US marines patrol Tikrit, the last stronghold of Saddam's regime

A Chinook helicopter hovers over the centre of Baghdad as allied soldiers try to restore order after the looting that followed liberation

Two marines stand by the artificial lake that surrounds Saddam's palace in Tikrit. Coalition troops met little resistance as they advanced

DESPATCH
15.04.03 FROM DAVID BLAIR IN BAGHDAD

YOU'VE BROKEN YOUR WORD, SAYS BAGHDAD BOY

Ali Ismail Abbas, the 12-year-old Baghdad boy who lost his arms in a US air strike, yesterday accused the media of letting him down.

He does not want sympathy. Speaking with fluent indignation, in his grimy ward in Chewader hospital, he demanded to know why numerous promises that he would be treated in the West had not been kept.

"The journalists always promise to evacuate me – why don't they do it now?" he asked, his brow furrowed with pain and glistening with sweat. "Please take me out of Iraq to be safe and cured."

An American bomb destroyed his home, in the suburb of Zafaranea, three weeks ago. He lost his mother, father, brother and two sisters.

The family were asleep when their home was turned into an inferno. Ali received second- and third-degree burns on his abdomen when his bedsheets caught fire. Shrapnel riddled his arms and both had to be amputated.

Day after day he has had to endure a bewildering succession of visitors from the international media. His wounds have been uncovered for cameramen and all have offered kind words.

Some have gone further and made specific promises. The *Daily Mirror* launched an appeal on Ali's behalf and the London *Evening Standard* used his face to launch their Red Cross "victims of war" appeal.

But the highly-intelligent articulate boy now has his doubts. "Are you coming to make fun of me because I have lost my arms?" he asked. "Doctor, doctor, no more journalists please."

Ali's condition is described as "critical but stable". The greatest danger would be septicaemia. If he is to be evacuated from Chewader hospital, this must be before infection takes hold. Dr Mowafak Gorea, the hospital's director, said, "We need realities, not dreams."

Ali has already been moved once, after looters ransacked one hospital. If he is to be moved again, Dr Gorea said air transport must be used and the swiftest route worked out. Thought must also be given to his six surviving sisters.

A doctor with the US marines in Baghdad said the American military was willing to evacuate Ali by air to Kuwait but no firm agreement had been reached with the hospital.

The immense pressure of work on Chewader hospital might help explain this. Of the six general hospitals in Baghdad, it is the only one still fully functioning.

Yesterday in the House of Commons, Tony Blair said, "We will do whatever we can to help him."

Two other Iraqi children had already been flown to Britain for treatment, he said, adding that they were in an area under British control.

Ali Ismail Abbas, aged 12, lying in pain on his bed in Baghdad's only fully functioning hospital, was critical of his treatment from members of the western media. 'Are you coming to make fun of me because I have lost my arms?' he asked. Later, he underwent a successful skin graft operation in Kuwait

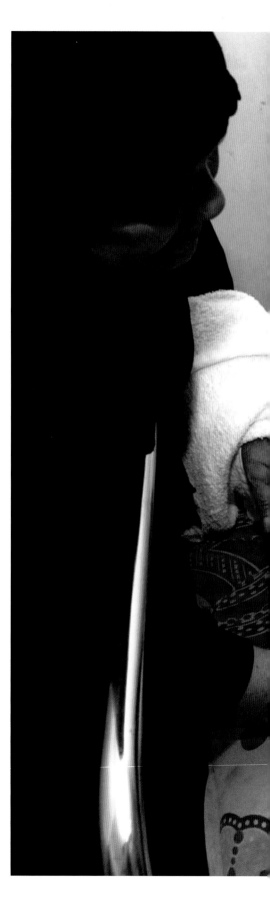

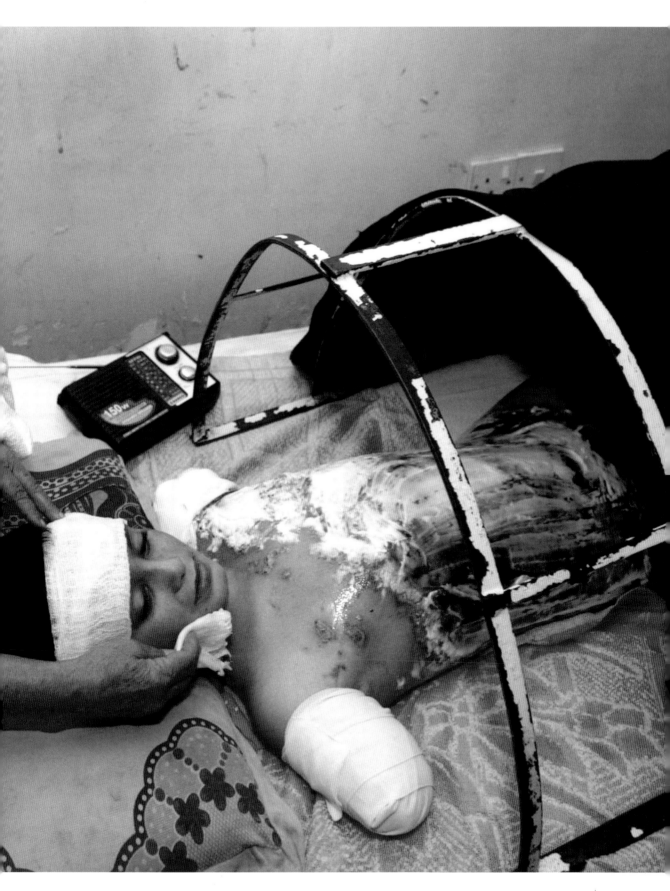

The land endures: Burnt-out cars and armoured vehicles may litter the Euphrates valley, but this verdant land, birthplace of civilisation, offers continual hope of a better future

THE MEDIA WAR
KIM FLETCHER ON HOW THE TV AND PRESS PERFORMED

A s American forces closed on the centre of Baghdad, television viewers in Britain and America cheered on the vehement claims of the Iraqi Information Minister.

"The infidels are committing suicide by the hundreds at the gates of Baghdad," said Mohammed Said al-Shahaf. "We made them drink poison last night. Be assured, Baghdad is safe."

The minister took to holding impromptu press conferences on the streets of the Iraqi capital. The more emphatic he became, the more we laughed. The joke was so funny because the pictures were so vivid. The television stations bringing us the information minister from the centre of Baghdad were also broadcasting pictures of American tanks from its suburbs. We could see for ourselves where truth lay.

"There are no American infidels in Baghdad. Never!" said the minister. At any moment, it seemed, a group of US marines would appear at his elbow.

The live television shots that followed over the next few days – American tanks rolling into Baghdad, a statue of Saddam Hussein toppled from its plinth, looting in the city streets – were the climax to a remarkable coverage of the war by all news media.

Here were American and British forces invading Iraq with hundreds of journalists travelling alongside them. Here were western journalists simultaneously reporting from the heart of the enemy capital. We watched this without surprise. Yet it was as if Adolf Hitler had invited British reporters into Berlin to report upon the last days of the Third Reich.

The opportunities for the media had not seemed so obvious when the war started. The coalition forces had invited news organisations to "embed" correspondents with American and British army, navy and air force units. About 900 reporters and photographers did so, joining units for training – including action

Iraqi information minister, Mohammed Said al-Shahaf, was given the soubriquet 'Comical Ali': His emphatic denials of allied successes were made immediately ridiculous by live footage of US tanks entering Baghdad

in the event of a chemical weapons attack – weeks before the conflict began. British correspondents embedded on the understanding that their copy would be made available to all papers.

The advantage of "embedding" was that it would bring many correspondents to the heart of the action under the protection of the military. The disadvantages were that journalists were in effect putting themselves under military jurisdiction, were unlikely to be free to write what they liked and were circumscribing their access to other areas of the conflict.

For that reason many news organisations hedged their bets by embedding some correspondents and instructing others to work as "unilaterals". Reuters, for example, had some 70 staff working in Iraq as the war progressed – 30 embedded and 40 working unilaterally. Unilaterals would be free to go where they liked – subject to getting themselves through checkpoints – and to write what they wanted. But they would have to look after themselves and faced considerable risks in driving into areas of the battlefield.

The risks were demonstrated when the ITN correspondent Terry Lloyd, working as a unilateral, died after becoming caught in fire believed to have come from American troops. His cameraman colleague, Fred Nerac, and the crew's interpreter, Hussein Osman, were reported missing after the same ambush.

Thirteen other journalists died during the war, not all as a result of military action. In addition, journalists stationed themselves in Kuwait – several TV companies decided to "anchor" their bulletins from Kuwait City – and Qatar, where the coalition forces set up a sophisticated media centre that they promised would convey all official information about the war.

Finally there was Baghdad. The Iraqi government, alert to the propaganda value of showing the world the civilian casualties of war, issued visas to most journalists who applied for them. It refused to allow in the BBC's John Simpson, who had reported from the capital during the last Gulf war and who had criticised the regime in a book. He nevertheless became one of some 200 BBC TV and radio correspondents and production staff in the region, covering the war from northern Iraq.

There were a number of concerns about working in the Iraqi capital: that journalists would be jeopardising their own safety; that they might be used by the Iraqi government as human shields; that their work would have propaganda value for the Iraqi regime. All journalists working in the city were required to do so under the close supervision of government minders, who would control their access to both places and people and monitor the content of their reports.

Many organised their own generators and emergency supplies, but there were doubts about the ability of television companies to get out pictures once the coalition air assault began. There were even rumours that the Americans had the ability to track and prevent the use of satellite links.

Some papers – including *The Daily Telegraph* and *The Times* – decided to withdraw correspondents, both for their own safety and to prevent their becoming human shields.

Three correspondents did die in Baghdad. A Reuters cameraman, Taras Protsyuk, 35, was killed when an American tank fired a shell at the 15th floor at the Palestine hotel, where many journalists were staying. Jose Couso, 37, a cameraman for the Spanish television channel Tele5, was wounded in the same attack and died later. An al-Jazeera cameraman, Tarek Ayyoub, 35, was killed when American bombs hit the satellite station's office.

The fears that correspondents might be killed or taken prisoner in Baghdad were to continue almost until the conclusion of the war. But within hours of the invasion's starting, it became clear that many other concerns about coverage had been groundless.

First, the lights did not go out in Baghdad.

Terry Lloyd, the ITN correspondent, died after being caught in crossfire, believed to have come from American troops

On the contrary, TV cameras positioned on hotel rooftops transmitted graphic pictures of the strategic bombardment of the city. Under the gaze of their Iraqi minders, correspondents were able to talk live on television and radio and to file to papers.

Second, those correspondents embedded with advancing coalition forces were able to file detailed reports of early action. There was no attempt by the coalition forces to delay this process with a complicated system of vetting. Correspondents knew what they could and couldn't say and practised self-censorship.

One who didn't, the Fox News presenter Geraldo Rivera, was escorted back to the Kuwaiti border after he drew a map in the sand to show his audience where the 101st Airborne was heading. "He went down in the sand and drew where the forces are going," said an official. "He gave away the big picture stuff."

This was certainly an extreme case. But it had already become clear that neither the Americans nor the British could entirely control the flow of information across the whole of the battlefront.

Early setbacks – the downing of a British Tornado and a fatal crash involving a British helicopter – were reported on British television and radio before the Ministry of Defence had had a chance to inform the servicemen's next of kin, leaving many families to fear for hours that their own sons or husbands had been killed.

Throughout the war, items of news – not all of them substantiated – were coming out through embedded correspondents and unilaterals and finding their way on air hours before they were confirmed or denied by officials in Qatar. Indeed, journalists based at the official press centre quickly became irritated by the shortage of hard detail.

Attention focused on the 24-hour, rolling news coverage provided by Sky TV, BBC 24, ITV News and the American news channels available through satellite and cable. The Qatar-based station, al-Jazeera, which caused controversy by broadcasting pictures of dead US servicemen, claimed to have doubled its subscriptions in Europe during the war.

While there was general agreement that the stations provided vivid pictures, there was concern that the need for constant, "real-time" action outweighed the benefits that analysis and interpretation might bring.

The coverage required correspondents to speak in generalisations from hotel rooftops, sometimes about matters of which they had no direct experience. Though they took care to stress that some of the news they reported was rumour rather than proven fact, they did not hesitate to pass it on. Episodes that looked dramatic on camera were played out live and at length, even if they had little importance in the greater scheme of the war.

On the first Sunday of the war, for example, the Sky audience was invited to watch for several hours as American tanks ended some Iraqi resistance on the outskirts of the port of Umm Qasr. As heavy shells destroyed Iraqi positions in front of a live, global audience, it was easy to overlook the fact that unseen Iraqi soldiers were being killed as we watched.

But there was no doubting the quality of the pictures, with astonishing images from the Baghdad skyline as the city came under nightly attack, dramatic scenes of action from the British around Basra and stirring stuff from Americans advancing on Baghdad.

Newspapers published compelling eyewitness reports from both embedded correspondents and those working independently. Competing with the live action of television, they also rediscovered the power of the photograph, whether in colour or black and white.

March 19, 2003

This was supposed to be a television war, but many believed that it was only in newspapers that they could find the analysis that made sense of the cascade of images they had seen on screen.

Once the war began, British papers took up the positions expected of them, with the *Sun*, in particular, becoming jingoistic in its coverage. The *Daily Mirror*, which had been outspoken in its criticism of America and Britain before the war, found it difficult to change tack. Its attempts to differentiate between its support for the coalition forces and its opposition to the coalition's policies was generally felt to be a failure, and the paper lost readers.

After initial circulation gains, most titles found it difficult to hold on to extra readers, though *The Guardian* and *The Independent* – which both opposed war – reported a small, continued growth.

The latter carried a series of reports from its experienced Middle East correspondent, Robert Fisk, in Baghdad, vilifying the coalition campaign. His view on the strength of defences in Baghdad was to prove inaccurate.

As the war progressed, there were accusa-

Constable & Robinson Ltd
3 The Lanchesters
162 Fulham Palace Road
London W6 9ER

www.constablerobinson.com

First published in the UK by Robinson, an imprint of Constable & Robinson Ltd, 2003

Copyright © Telegraph Group Limited 2003
The Secret War copyright © Michael Smith 2003

A copy of the British Library Cataloguing in Publication Data is available from the British Library

ISBN 1-84119-839-0

Printed and bound in the UK by Butler & Tanner

The Daily Telegraph

Creative Director
Clive Crook

Editorial Projects Director
George Darby

Designer
Mark Hickling

Picture Editor
Abi Patton

Text Editor
Richard Parrack

Picture assistant
Claudia Baistow

Maps and Drawings
Daily Telegraph Graphics

Publisher,
Telegraph Books
Morven Knowles

Reproduction
Graphic Facilities, London

With thanks to the editors, staff and correspondents of *The Daily Telegraph*, particularly to Alec Russell, Foreign Editor, and Bob Bodman, Picture Editor

tions that other journalists were failing to report with objectivity. When the campaign briefly appeared to have slowed, many commentators reported that it was clearly bogged down, that Iraq was to be a latter-day Vietnam and that the Iraqi regime would defend Baghdad with the ferocity shown by the Russians in Stalingrad.

The BBC was singled out for criticism – not least by *The Daily Telegraph* – on the basis that it talked up gloom about the coalition advance and showed anti-war and anti-American bias in its reports. The corporation's own defence correspondent, Paul Adams, e-mailed colleagues from Qatar, accusing them of exaggerating the problems faced by coalition forces.

At the end of the war, Greg Dyke, the BBC director general, rejected criticism. He claimed the corporation had received hundreds of e-mails praising its questioning approach.

But did the media bring home a full picture of the war? In terms of providing an accurate, overall picture of what was going on at any time, yes they did. They may have reported the fall of Umm Qasr every day for three

April 3, 2003

days until it finally fell. They may have underestimated – and then exaggerated – difficulties in Basra. They may have been too forward in announcing the big move on Baghdad. Yet, as the war progressed, we, the public, had a pretty good idea of the big picture, even if we were viewing, hearing and reading only fragments of action, vivid parts of a bigger jigsaw.

Whole areas of conflict – the work of the Special Forces, for instance – went completely unseen.

And though we knew, day by day, the way that things were going, we deluded ourselves if we thought we were seeing war in the raw. This was a sanitised version.

How many Iraqis died? Who knows? It is a question that the media were unable to answer and, while there were photographs and video footage of Iraqi corpses available, most newspapers declined to show them. At no time in this conflict did we see the kind of searing images that were published in 1991, after American planes attacked Iraqi forces retreating from Kuwait.

Did events like this not happen this time? Or is it simply that no one was there to record them?

TOP 20 PLAYERS IN THE POWER GAME THAT LED TO THE INVASION OF IRAQ

The weeks of war were preceded by months of diplomatic wrangling at the United Nations Security Council. It started with the reports to the council by the head of the UN inspection teams, Hans Blix. His reports failed to provide America with the 'smoking gun'. Undeterred, Britain and (to a lesser extent) America, pushed hard to gain UN backing for war. But the so-called 'Axis of Weasel' — France, Germany and Russia, dashed the allies' hopes. In the end, Britain and America, joined by Australia and Poland, overthrew Saddam's regime on their own

6 Colin Powell, US Secretary of State
A former general who served with the first President Bush, Mr Powell was seen by many as a moderating influence on the hawkish second Bush administration.

1 President Saddam Hussein
One of the last of the 20th century's notorious dictators, Saddam staked everything on dividing western opinion, playing one leader off the other, but in the end underestimated Anglo-US resolve to see him thrown out of power.

2 President George W Bush
Overshadowed going into the conflict by suggestions he was in thrall to his father's old advisers, President Bush ended the war with his reputation greatly enhanced. But, as with his father, there are questions about his skills at handling the economy.

3 Tony Blair, the Prime Minister
He staked his political future on the war and was prepared to resign if the House of Commons failed to back him. It did. He emerged from the conflict as America's No 1 ally, but his relationship with Britain's European allies took a severe mauling.

4 Jacques Chirac, President of France
President Chirac's obstruction of any UN mandate to authorise force won him unprecedented popularity in France, but at a huge cost in Franco-US political relations.

5 Donald Rumsfeld, US Defence Secretary
Determined to drive through his programme of reform in the Pentagon, Mr Rumsfeld was chief advocate for the relatively light forces that America deployed.

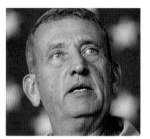

7 General Tommy Franks, Commander Centcom
Gen Frank's original plan for a heavy land force was thrown out by Mr Rumsfeld. However, Gen Franks skillfully used the much smaller forces to brilliant effect.

8 Hans Blix, Chief Unmovic
The former Swedish diplomat irritated the Bush White House by refusing to condemn the Iraqi regime for its illegal chemical and biological weapons programme.

9 Mohammed al-Sahaf 'Comical Ali'

The Iraqi infomation minister became a figure of derision for his florid predictions of American disaster. After the war he was signed up by an Arab TV station.

12 Jack Straw Foreign Secretary

His resolute performance in the United Nations, attacking his French counterpart, won him many plaudits, but he was ultimately over-shadowed by Tony Blair.

15 Sir Jeremy Greenstock, UK's UN ambassador

A skilled diplomat, the urbane former Assistant Master of Eton was the driving force behind the allies' attempts at securing UN backing for the use of force against Saddam.

18 Gen Richard Myers, US Chairman of the Joint Chief of Staff

A former pilot, Gen Myers was a keen supporter of Mr Rumsfeld's plan to use air power to replace soldiers on the ground.

10 Gerhard Schröder, German Chancellor

Mr Schröder went against years of German foreign policy in opposing America. Relations between Washington and Berlin have been frosty ever since.

13 John Howard, Australia's PM

Like Mr Blair, Mr Howard risked his political future in backing Mr Bush. His support for the war was deeply unpopular at home but he secured America's long-term friendship.

16 Kofi Annan, UN Secretary-General

Unable to bridge the gulf that existed in the Security Council, Mr Annan presided over one of the most serious crises in the history of the United Nations.

19 Aleksander Kwasniewski, President of Poland

The forgotten ally, Poland was one of only two other countries to send ground troops into Iraq. Poland should be a winner in the shake-up of US forces in Europe.

11 Tariq Aziz, Deputy PM of Iraq

The only Christian in Saddam's inner circle, Aziz had become the best-known member of the Iraqi regime. He was captured at the end of the war.

14 Vladimir Putin, President of Russia

Mr Putin joined Mr Schröder and M Chirac in the 'Axis of Weasel', vigorously opposing the use of force against Iraq.

17 Air Marshal Brian Burridge, British commander

Britain's commander in the war, and the overall coalition deputy commander, the former Nimrod pilot attacked the British media for its coverage during the war.

20 Jose Maria Aznar, PM of Spain

The political ally of Britain and America, Aznar went against strong domestic opinion to provide unwavering diplomatic support for the Anglo-US alliance.

THE DEADLY ARSENAL OF THE WAR

It was a one-sided war. The technological superiority enjoyed by the western allies meant that the crumbling Iraqi army was totally overwhelmed.

B52 Stratofortress
United States
Wingspan: 185ft
Bomb load: 18 satellite-guided JDAM or 20 AGM86C air-launched cruise missiles
Crew: 5
Notes: The Vietnam-era bomber has been given a new lease of life with the introduction of new precision-guided munitions

AH64D Apache
United States
Crew: 2
Wingspan: 17.15ft
Main armament: Hellfire anti-tank missiles, 30mm cannon, 70mm folding-fin aerial rockets
Notes: Star of the 1991 Gulf war, the Apache proved less effective in 2003. One raid by up to 40 helicopters was ambushed, with 30 of the aircraft being damaged by small arms fire and salvo after salvo of RPG7 grenades

E3 Sentry (Awacs)
United States
Wingspan: 130ft
Crew: 4+ 13-19 specialists
Main armament: nil
Notes: The Sentry is an airborne warning and control system that provided all-weather command, control and communications for air operations over Iraq

F117A Nighthawk
United States
Wingspan: 43ft
Bomb load: two each of Mk84 2000lb, GBU10, GBU12, GBU27
Crew: 1
Notes: The world's first stealth attack aircraft was used on the first night of the war in a strike against Saddam's bunker

CVN75
USS Harry S Truman
United States
Displacement: 87,000 tons
Crew: 5,680
Weapon systems: 60+ aircraft
Notes: One of three nuclear-powered carriers on station around the Gulf, each with a Carrier Air Wing of at least four attack squadrons. The carriers were accompanied by a battle group of around 10 other ships, including submarines

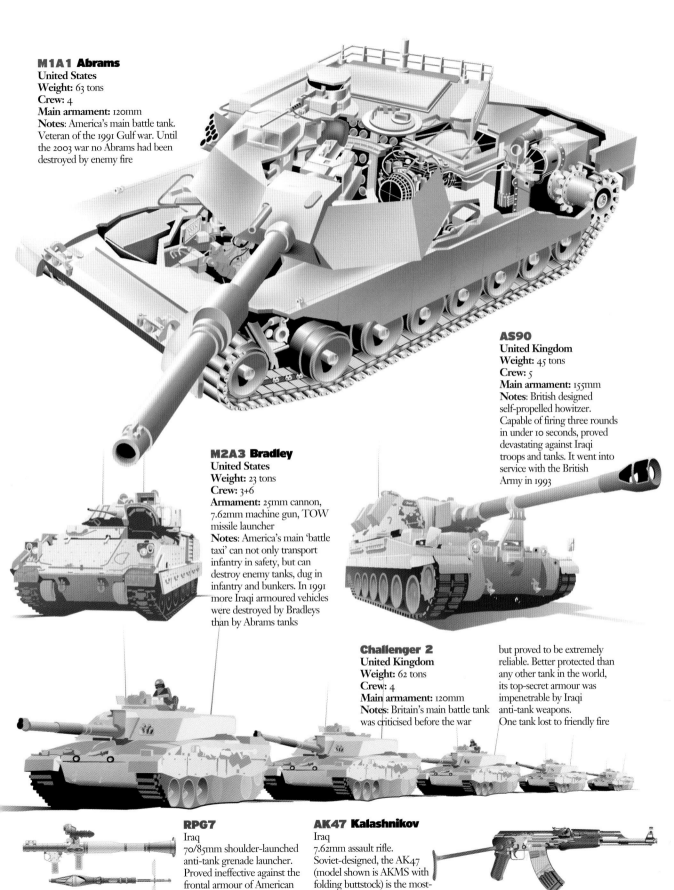

M1A1 Abrams
United States
Weight: 63 tons
Crew: 4
Main armament: 120mm
Notes: America's main battle tank. Veteran of the 1991 Gulf war. Until the 2003 war no Abrams had been destroyed by enemy fire

AS90
United Kingdom
Weight: 45 tons
Crew: 5
Main armament: 155mm
Notes: British designed self-propelled howitzer. Capable of firing three rounds in under 10 seconds, proved devastating against Iraqi troops and tanks. It went into service with the British Army in 1993

M2A3 Bradley
United States
Weight: 23 tons
Crew: 3+6
Armament: 25mm cannon, 7.62mm machine gun, TOW missile launcher
Notes: America's main 'battle taxi' can not only transport infantry in safety, but can destroy enemy tanks, dug in infantry and bunkers. In 1991 more Iraqi armoured vehicles were destroyed by Bradleys than by Abrams tanks

Challenger 2
United Kingdom
Weight: 62 tons
Crew: 4
Main armament: 120mm
Notes: Britain's main battle tank was criticised before the war but proved to be extremely reliable. Better protected than any other tank in the world, its top-secret armour was impenetrable by Iraqi anti-tank weapons. One tank lost to friendly fire

RPG7
Iraq
70/85mm shoulder-launched anti-tank grenade launcher. Proved ineffective against the frontal armour of American and British tanks

AK47 Kalashnikov
Iraq
7.62mm assault rifle. Soviet-designed, the AK47 (model shown is AKMS with folding buttstock) is the most-exported rifle in the world

BRITISH SERVICEMEN KILLED IN IRAQ

Some 33 British servicemen were killed during Operation Telic, the British name for Operation Iraqi Freedom. Of those, seven were serving with the Royal Navy, eight with the Royal Marines, 16 with the British Army and two with the Royal Air Force.

Six servicemen are listed by the Ministry of Defence as being killed in action. The others died in accidents or as a result of so-called 'friendly-fire' incidents.

Warrant Officer Second Class Mark Stratford, 39, serving with the Royal Marines

Corporal Stephen John Allbutt, 35, from Stoke-on-Trent, Staffs, serving with the Queen's Royal Lancers

Sergeant Steven Mark Roberts, 33, from Bradford, West Yorkshire serving with 2nd Royal Tank Regiment

Flight Lieutenant Kevin Main, 37, from Bruntwood, Staffs, serving with 9 Squadron Royal Air Force

Trooper David Jeffrey Clarke, 19, from Littleworth, Staffs, serving with the Queen's Royal Lancers

Flight Lieutenant Dave Rhys Williams, 37, from Crickhowell, Powys, serving with 9 Squadron Royal Air Force

Lance Corporal of Horse Matty Hull, 25, from Windsor, Berks, serving with The Blues & Royals, Household Cavalry Regiment

Lance Corporal Barry Stephen, 31, from Scone, Perthshire, serving with the 1st Battalion, The Black Watch

Lieutenant James Williams, 28, from Falmouth, Cornwall, serving with 849 Squadron, Royal Navy

Lance Corporal James McCue, 27, from Paisley, Renfrewshire, serving with 7 Air Assault Battalion, Royal Electrical and Mechanical Engineers

Lance Corporal Shaun Andrew Brierley, 28, based in Herford, Germany, serving with 212 Signal Squadron, 1 (UK) Armoured Division HQ & Signal Regiment

Staff Sergeant Simon Cullingworth, 36, from Essex, serving with 33 (EOD) Engineer Regiment, a specialist bomb disposal unit based at Carver Barracks, Essex

Sapper Luke Allsopp, 24, from north London, serving with 33 (EOD) Engineer Regiment, a specialist bomb disposal unit based at Carver Barracks, Essex

Lieutenant Philip West, 32, of Budock Water, near Falmouth, Cornwall, serving with 849 Squadron, Royal Navy

Lieutenant Andrew Wilson, 36, based at Culdrose, Cornwall, serving with 849 Squadron, Royal Navy

Marine Sholto Hedenskog, 26, from South Africa, serving with the Royal Marines

Colour Sergeant John Cecil, from Plymouth, serving with the Royal Marines

Sergeant Les Hehir, 34, of Poole, Dorset, serving with the Royal Marines

Lieutenant Philip D Green, 31, from Prestwick, Ayrshire, serving with 849 Squadron, Royal Navy

Captain Philip Guy, 29, from Bishopdale, North Yorkshire, serving with the Royal Marines

Major Jason Ward, 34, of Heavitree, Exeter, serving with the Royal Marines

Lance Corporal Ian Keith Malone, 28, from Dublin, serving with the Irish Guards

Major Stephen Alexis Ballard, 3 Commando Brigade, serving with the Royal Marines

Lieutenant Marc Lawrence, 26, from Westgate, Kent, serving with 849 Squadron, Royal Navy

Lieutenant Antony King, 35, of Helston, Cornwall, serving with 849 Squadron, Royal Navy

Fusilier Kelan John Turrington, 18, from Haslingfield, Cambridgeshire, serving with the Royal Regiment of Fusiliers

Piper Christopher Muzvuru, 21, from Gweru, Zimbabwe, serving with the Irish Guards

Staff Sergeant Chris Muir, 32, from Romsey, Hampshire, serving with the Army School of Ammunition, Royal Logistic Corps

Operator Mechanic (Communications) Second Class Ian Seymour RN, 29, from Poole, Dorset, serving with 148 Commando Battery Royal Artillery

Marine Christopher R Maddison, 24, from Scarborough, North Yorkshire, serving with 9 Assault Squadron Royal Marines

Lance Bombardier Llywelyn Karl Evans, 24, from Llandudno, North Wales, serving with 29 Commando Regiment Royal Artillery

Lance Corporal Karl Shearer, 24, from Windsor, Berkshire, serving with The Blues and Royals, Household Cavalry Regiment

Lieutenant Alexander Tweedie, 25, from Minto, Hawick, serving with The Blues and Royals, Household Cavalry Regiment

US SERVICE PERSONNEL KILLED IN IRAQ

Army Pfc.
John E. Brown, 21.
Army Spc.
Thomas A. Foley III.
Marine Cpl.
Armando Ariel Gonzalez. 25.
Army Spc.
Richard A. Goward, 32.
Army Pfc.
Joseph P. Mayek, 20.
Army Spc.
Gil Mercado, 25.
Marine Cpl.
Jesus A. Gonzalez, 22.
Marine Lance Cpl.
David Edward Owens Jr.
Staff Sgt.
Riayan A. Tejeda, 26.
Marine Gunnery Sgt.
Jeffrey E. Bohr Jr., 39.
Army Staff Sgt.
Terry W. Hemingway, 39.
Army Cpl.
Henry L. Brown, 22.
Marine Pfc.
Juan Guadalupe Garza Jr., 20.
Army Sgt. 1st Class
John W. Marshall, 50.
Army Pfc.
Jason M. Meyer, 23.
Air Force Staff Sgt.
Scott D. Sather, 29.
Army Staff Sgt.
Robert A. Stever, 36.
Marine Lance Cpl.
Andrew Julian Aviles, 18.
Army Staff Sgt.
Lincoln D. Hollinsaid, 27.
Army 2nd Lt.
Jeffrey J. Kaylor, 24.
Marine Cpl.
Jesus Martin Antonio Medellin, 21.
Army Pfc.
Anthony S. Miller, 19.

Army Spc.
George A. Mitchell, 35.
Army Pfc.
Gregory P. Huxley Jr., 19.
Army Pvt.
Kelley S. Prewitt, 24.
Army Staff Sgt.
Stevon A. Booker, 34.
Army Spc.
Larry K. Brown, 22.
Marine 1st Sgt.
Edward Smith, 38.
Army Capt.
Tristan N. Aitken, 31.
Army Pfc.
Wilfred D. Bellard, 20.
Army Spc.
Daniel Francis J. Cunningham, 33.
Marine Capt.
Travis A. Ford, 30.
Marine Cpl.
Bernard G. Gooden, 22.
Army Pvt.
Devon D. Jones, 19.
Marine 1st Lt.
Brian M. McPhillips, 25.
Marine Sgt.
Duane R. Rios, 25.
Marine Capt.
Benjamin W. Sammis, 29.
Army Sgt. 1st Class
Paul R. Smith, 33.
Marine Pfc.
Chad E. Bales, 20.
Army Staff Sgt.
Wilbert Davis, 40.
Marine Cpl.
Mark A. Evnin, 21.
Army Capt.
Edward J. Korn, 31.
Army Staff Sgt.
Nino D. Livaudais, 23.
Army Spc.
Ryan P. Long, 21.
Army Spc.
Donald S. Oaks Jr., 20.

Army Sgt. 1st Class
Randall S. Rehn, 36.
Army Capt.
Russell B. Rippetoe, 27.
Army Sgt.
Todd J. Robbins, 33.
Marine Cpl.
Erik H. Silva, 22.
Army Capt.
James F. Adamouski, 29.
Marine Lance Cpl.
Brian E. Anderson, 26.
Army Spc.
Mathew G. Boule, 22.
Army Master Sgt.
George A. Fernandez, 36.
Marine Pfc.
Christian D. Gurtner, 19.
Army Chief Warrant Officer 4
Erik A. Halvorsen, 40.
Army Chief Warrant Officer
Scott Jamar, 32.
Army Sgt.
Michael F. Pedersen, 26.
Army Chief Warrant Officer
Eric A. Smith, 41.
Navy Lt.
Nathan D. White, 30.
Army Sgt.
Jacob L. Butler, 24.
Marine Lance Cpl.
Joseph B. Maglione, 22.
Army Spc.
Brandon J. Rowe, 20.
Marine Capt.
Aaron J. Contreras, 31.
Marine Sgt.
Michael V. Lalush, 23.
Marine Sgt.
Brian McGinnis, 23.
Marine Staff Sgt.
James W.Cawley, 41.
Army Spc.
Michael Edward Curtin, 23.
Army Pfc.
Diego Fernando Rincon, 19.
Army Pfc.
Michael Russell Creighton Weldon, 20.
Marine Lance Cpl.
William W. White, 24.
Army Sgt.
Eugene Williams, 24.

Army Sgt.
Roderic A. Solomon, 32.
Marine Gunnery Sgt.
Joseph Menusa, 33.
Marine Cpl.
Robert M. Rodriguez, 21.
Marine Lance Cpl.
Jesus A. Suarez Del Solar, 20.
Army Spc.
William A. Jeffries, 39.
Marine Maj.
Kevin Nave, 36.
Marine Pfc.
Francisco A. Martinez-Flores, 21.
Navy Hospital Corpsman 3rd Class
Michael Vann Johnson Jr., 25.
Marine Staff Sgt.
Donald C. May Jr., 31.
Marine Lance Cpl.
Patrick T. O'Day, 20.
Marine Lance Cpl.
Thomas A. Blair, 24.
Marine Cpl.
Evan T. James, 20.
Marine Sgt.
Bradley S. Korthaus, 28.
Army Spc.
Gregory P. Sanders, 19.
Air National Guard Maj.
Gregory Stone, 40.
Army Spc.
Jamaal R. Addison, 22.
Marine Sgt.
Michael E. Bitz, 31.
Marine Lance Cpl.
Brian Rory Buesing, 20.
Army Sgt. George
Edward Buggs, 31.
Marine Pfc.
Tamario D. Burkett, 21.
Marine Cpl.
Kemaphoom A. Chanawongse, 22.
Marine Lance Cpl.
Donald J. Cline Jr., 21.
Army Master Sgt.
Robert J. Dowdy, 38.
Army Pvt.
Ruben Estrella-Soto, 18.
Marine Lance Cpl.
David K. Fribley, 26.
Marine Cpl.
Jose A. Garibay, 21.

Marine Pvt.
Jonathan L. Gifford, 20.
Marine Sgt.
Fernando Padilla-Ramirez, 26.
Marine Cpl.
Jorge A. Gonzalez, 20.
Marine Pvt.
Nolen R. Hutchings, 19.
Army Pfc.
Howard Johnson II, 21.
Marine Staff Sgt.
Phillip A. Jordan, 42.
Army Spc.
James M. Kiehl, 22.
Army Chief Warrant Officer
Johnny Villareal Mata, 35.
Marine Lance Cpl.
Patrick R. Nixon, 21.
Army Pfc.
Lori Ann Piestewa, 23.
Marine 2nd Lt.
Frederick E. Pokorney Jr., 31.
Marine Sgt.
Brendon C. Reiss, 23.
Marine Cpl.
Randal Kent Rosacker, 21.
Army Pvt.
Brandon Ulysses Sloan, 19.
Marine Lance Cpl.
Thomas J. Slocum, 22.
Army Sgt.
Donald Ralph Walters, 33.
Marine Lance Cpl.
Michael J. Williams, 31.
Navy Lt.
Thomas Mullen Adams, 27.
Marine Sgt.
Nicolas M. Hodson, 22.
Marine Lance Cpl.
Eric J. Orlowski, 26.
Army Capt.
Christopher Scott Seifert, 27.
Army Reserve Spc.
Brandon S. Tobler, 19.
Marine 2nd Lt.
Therrel S. Childers, 30.
Marine Lance Cpl.
Jose Gutierrez, 22.
Army Sgt.
Edward J. Anguiano, 24.

FORCES THAT TOOK PART IN THE WAR

UK

ROYAL NAVY AND ROYAL MARINES
Rear Admiral David Snelson
HMS Ark Royal (aircraft carrier)
HMS Ocean (helicopter carrier)
HMS Liverpool (Type 42 destroyer)
HMS Edinburgh (Type 42 destroyer)
HMS York (Type 42 destroyer)
HMS Marlborough (Type 23 frigate)
HMS Richmond (Type 23 frigate)
HMS Grimsby (minehunter)
HMS Ledbury (minehunter)
HMS Brocklesby (minehunter)
HMS Blyth (minehunter)
HMS Chatham (Type 22 frigate)
HMS Splendid
(Swiftsure class submarine)
HMS Turbulent
(Trafalgar class submarine)
RFA Argus
RFA Sir Tristram
RFA Sir Galahad
RFA Sir Percivale
RFA Fort Victoria
RFA Fort Rosalie
RFA Fort Austin
RFA Orangeleaf

The amphibious force
Commodore Jamie Miller
numbers some 4,000 and includes:

HQ 3 Commando Brigade
Brigadier James Dutton
40 Commando Royal Marines
42 Commando Royal Marines
45 Commando Royal Marines
29 Regt, Royal Artillery
(105mm Light Gun)
539 Assault Sqn, RM
59 Commando Sqn, RE

Helicopter air groups aboard Ark Royal and Ocean including:
845, 846, 847, 849 Sqns

ARMY
Major General Robin Brims
1 (UK) Armoured Division:
Headquarters and 1 Armoured
Division Signal Regt
30 Signal Regt
(strategic communications)
The Queen's Dragoon Guards
(reconnaissance)
1st Bn The Duke of Wellington's
Regt (additional infantry capability)
28 Engineer Regt
1 General Support Regt,
Royal Logistic Corps
2 Close Support Regt,
Royal Logistic Corps
2nd Bn, Royal Electrical &
Mechanical Engineers
1 Close Support Medical Regt
5 General Support Medical Regt
1 Regt, Royal Military Police
plus elements from various units
including:
33 Explosive Ordnance Disposal Regt
30 Signal Regt
32 Regt Royal Artillery
(Phoenix UAVs)

7th Armoured Brigade
Brigadier Graham Binns
Headquarters and Signal Sqn:
Royal Scots Dragoon Guards
(Challenger 2 tanks)
2nd Royal Tank Regt
(Challenger 2 tanks)
1st Bn The Black Watch
(Warrior infantry fighting vehicles)
1st Bn Royal Regt of Fusiliers
(Warrior infantry fighting vehicles)
3rd Regt Royal Horse Artillery
(AS90 self-propelled guns)
32 Armoured Engineer Regt
plus elements from various units
including:
Queen's Royal Lancers
(Challenger 2 tanks)
1st Bn Irish Guards
(Warrior infantry fighting vehicles)
1st Bn The Light Infantry
(Warrior infantry fighting vehicles)
26 Regt Royal Artillery
38 Engineer Regt

---

16 Air Assault Brigade
Brigader Jacko Page
Headquarters and Signal Sqn
1st Bn The Royal Irish Regt
1st Bn The Parachute Regt
3rd Bn The Parachute Regt
7 (Para) Regt Royal Horse Artillery
(105mm Light Guns)
23 Engineer Regt
D sqn, Household Cavalry Regt
3 Regt Army Air Corps
(Lynx & Gazelle helicopters)
7 Air Assault Bn, Royal Electrical &
Mechanical Engineers
13 Air Assault Support Regt,
Royal Logistic Corps
16 Close Support Medical Regt
156 Provost Company RMP

102 Logistics Brigade
Brigadier Shaun Cowlan
Headquarters 2 Signal Regt
36 Engineer Regt
33 and 34 Field Hospitals
202 Field Hospital (Volunteer)
4 General Support Medical Regt
3 Bn, Royal Electrical & Mechanical
Engineers
6 Supply Regt, Royal Logistic Corps
7 Transport Regt, Royal Logistic
Corps
17 Port & Maritime Regt, Royal
Logistic Corps
23 Pioneer Regt, Royal Logistic
Corps
24 Regt, Royal Logistic Corps
5 Regt, Royal Military Police
specialist Royal Engineer teams
airfield engineer support units from
12 Engineer Brigade
elements from 11 Explosive
Ordnance Disposal Regt
elements from additional Royal
Logistic Corps Regts

ROYAL AIR FORCE
Air Vice Marshal Glenn Torpy
Composite sqns formed
including elements from:

9, 13, 31, 39 (1 PRU) Sqns, RAF
Marham
12, 14, 617 Sqns, RAF Lossiemouth
11, 25 Sqns, RAF Leeming
43, 111 Sqns, RAF Leuchars
6, 41, 54 Sqns, RAF Coltishall
1, 3, IV Sqns, RAF Cottesmore

UK

8, 23, 51 Sqns, RAF Waddington
33 Sqn, RAF Benson
10, 99, 101, 216 Sqns, RAF Brize Norton
24, 30, 47, 70 Sqns, RAF Lyneham
120, 201, 206 Sqns, RAF Kinloss
7, 18, 27 Sqns, RAF Odiham
RAF Regt

AUSTRALIA

NAVY
HMAS Kanimbla
HMAS Anzac
HMAS Darwin

AIRFORCE
one RAAF sqn F/A 18
three RAAF C130
two P3C Orion

ARMY
Special forces task group including SAS, and 4 Royal Australian Regt

POLAND

200 special forces

USA
Elements included

US ARMY
Special Operations Command
5th Special Forces Group
75th Ranger Regt
160th Special Ops Aviation Regt

3rd Infantry Division
1st Bn, 39th Fd Artillery Regt
11th Aviation Regt
1st Brigade
  2nd, 3rd Bns, 7th Infantry Regt
  3rd Bn, 69th Armor Regt
  1st Bn, 41st Fd Artillery Regt
2nd Brigade
  3rd Bn, 15th Infantry Regt
  1st, 4th Bns, 64th Armor Regt
  E Troop, 9th Cavalry Regt
  1st Bn, 9th Fd Artillery Regt
3rd Brigade
  1st Bn, 30th Infantry Regt
  1st Bn, 15th Infantry Regt
  2nd Bn, 69th Armor Regt
  D Troop, 10th Cavalry Regt
  1st Bn, 10th Fd Artillery Regt
Aviation Brigade
  1st Bn, 3rd Aviation Regt
  2nd Bn, 3rd Aviation Regt
  3rd Sqn, 7th Cavalry Regt

82nd Airborne Division
2nd Brigade Combat Team
  1st, 2nd, 3rd Bns, 325th Airborne Infantry
1st Bn, 82nd Aviation Regt

101st Airborne Division
1st Brigade, 101st Airborne Division
  1st, 2nd, 3rd Bns, 327th Infantry Regt
2nd Brigade, 101st Airborne Division
  1st, 2nd, 3rd Bns, 502nd Infantry Regt
3rd Brigade, 101st Airborne Division
  1st, 2nd, 3rd Bns, 187th Infantry Regt
101st Aviation Brigade
  2nd Bn, 17th Cavalry Regt
  1st, 2nd, 3rd, 6th Bns, 101st Aviation Regt
159th Aviation Brigade
  4th, 5th, 7th, 9th Bns, 101st Aviation Regt
Divarty
  1st, 2nd, 3rd Bns,

320th Fd Artillery Regt

173rd Airborne Brigade
  1st, 2nd Bns, 508th Infantry
  173rd Engineer Detachment
  173rd Brigade Recon Company
  Battery D, 3rd Bn, 319th Airborne Fd Artillery,

US MARINE CORPS
1 Marine Expeditionary Force
1st Marine Division
1st Marine Regt
  3rd Bn, 1st Marines
  1st Bn, 4th Marines
  1st, 3rd Bns, Light Armored Recon
5th Marine Regt
  1st Bn, 5th Marines.
  2nd, 3rd Bns, 5th Marines
7th Marine Regt
  1st, 3rd Bns, 7th Marines
  3rd Bn, 4th Marines
  3rd Bn, 11th Marines
  1st Tank Bn

2nd Marine Expeditionary Brigade, **2nd Marine Division**
  1st, 3rd Bns, 2nd Marines
  2nd Bn, 8th Marines
  1st Bn, 10th Marines
  2nd Amphibious Assault Bn
  2nd Recon Bn
  2nd Light Armored Recon Bn
  2nd, 8th Tank Bns

15th Marine Expeditionary Unit

24th Marine Expeditionary Unit

26th Marine Expeditionary Unit

US AIRFORCE
Special Ops
16th Special Ops Wing (AC130)
20th Special Ops Sqn (MH53M)
193rd Special Ops Wing (EC130E)

Ali Al Salem AB, Kuwait
386th Air Exped Group
118th Fighter Sqn (A10)
41st Electronic Combat Sqn (EC130)

Al Jaber AB, Kuwait
332nd Air Exped Group
52nd Fighter Wing

22nd, 23rd Fighter Sqns (F16)
172nd Fighter Sqn (A10)
332nd Exped Air Support Ops Sqn
332nd Exped Intelligence Flight
332nd Exped Rescue Sqn (HH60G)
552nd Air Control Wing (E3 Awacs)

Masirah AB, Oman
355th Air Exped Group
4th Special Ops Sqn (AC130U)
8th Special Ops Sqn (MC130E)

Thumrait AB, Oman
405th Air Exped Wing
405th Exped Bomb Sqn (B1B)
28th, 34th, 37th Bomb Wings (B1B)
55th Wing (RC135)

Al Udeid AB, Qatar
379th Air Exped Wing
49th Fighter Wing (F117)
4th Ops Group (F15)
336th Fighter Sqn (F15)
93rd Air Control Wing (E8 Jstars)

Al Dhafra AB, UAE
380th Air Exped Wing
9th, 57th Recon Wings (U2)
11th, 12th, 15th Recon Sqn (RQ1A)

Prince Sultan AB, Saudi Arabia
363rd Air Exped Wing
14th, 22nd Fighter Sqns (F16)
67th, 390th Fighter Sqns (F15)
457th, 524th Fighter Sqns (F16)
363 Exped Airborne Air Control Sqn
(E3 AWACS)
38th Recon Sqn (RC135)
99th Recon Sqn (U2)
VAQ-142 (EA6B)

Diego Garcia
40th Air Exped Wing
509th Bomb Wing
20th, 40th Bomb Sqns (B2)

RAF Fairford, United Kingdom
457th Air Exped Group
23rd Bomb Sqn (B52)
509th Bomb Wing
9th Recon Wing

US NAVY
**Theodore Roosevelt Carrier
Battle Group**
USS Theodore Roosevelt (CVN 71)
Carrier Air Wing 8

USS Anzi (CG 68)
USS Cape St. George (CG 71)
USS Arleigh Burke (DDG 51)
USS Porter (DDG 78)
USS Winston Churchill (DDG 81)
USS Stump (DD 978)
USS Carr (FFG 52)
USS Arctic (AOE 8)

**Harry S Truman Carrier
Battle Group**
USS Harry S Truman (CVN 75
Carrier Air Wing 3
USS San Jacint (CG 56)
USS Oscar Austin (DDG 79)
USS Mitscher (DDG 57)
USS Donald Cook (DDG 75)
USS Briscoe (DD 977)
USS Dey (DD 989)
USS Hawes (FFG 53)
USNS Kanawha (T-A196)
USNS Mount Baker (T-AE 34)
USS Pittsburgh (SSN 720)
USS Montpelier (SSN 765)

Kitty Hawk Carrier Battle Group
USS Kitty Hawk (CV 63)
Carrier Air Wing 5
USS Chancellorsville (CG 62)
USS Cowpens (CG 63)
USS John S. McCain (DDG 56)
USS O'Brien (DD 975)
USS Cushing (DD 985)
USS Vandergrift (FFG 48)
USS Gary (FFG 51)
USS Bremerton (SSN 698)

**Abraham Lincoln Carrier
Battle Group**
USS Abraham Lincoln (CVN 72)
Carrier Air Wing 14
USS Mobile Bay (CG 53)
USS Shiloh (CG 67)
USS Paul Hamilton (DDG 60)
USS Fletcher (DD 992)
USS Crommlein (FFG 37)
USS Reuben James (FFG 57)
USS Camden (AOE 2)
USS Honolulu (SSN 718)
USS Cheyenne (SSN 773)

Constellation Carrier Battle Group
USS Constellation (CV 64)
Carrier Air Wing 2
USS Valley Forge (CG 50)
USS Bunker Hill (CG 52)
USS Higgins (DDG 76)
USS Thach (FFG 43)

USS Ranier (AOE 7)
USS Columbia (SSN 771)
USS Milius (DDG 69)

Nimitz Carrier Battle Group
USS Nimitz (CVN 68)
Carrier Air Wing 11
USS Princeton (CG 59)
USS Chosin (G 65)
USS Fitzgerald (DDG 62)
USS Benfold (DDG 65)
USS Oldendorf (DD 972)
USS Rodney M. Davis (FFG 60)
USS Pasadena (SSN 752)
USS Bridge (AOE-10)

Amphibious Task Force East
USS Saipan (LHA 2)
USS Gunston Hall (LSD 44)
USS Ponce (LPD 15)
USS Bataan (LHD 5)
USS Kearsarge (LHD 3)
USS Ashland (LSD 48)
USS Portland (LSD 37)
Marine Aircraft Group 29

Amphibious Task Force West
USS Boxer (LHD 4)
USS Bonhomme Richard (LHD 6)
USS Cleveland (LPD 7)
USS Dubuque (LPD 8)
USS Anchorage (LSD 36)
USS Comstock (LSD 45)
USS Pearl Harbor (LSD 52)

Tarawa Amphibious Ready Group
USS Tarawa (LHA 1)
USS Duluth (LPD 6)
USS Rushmore (LSD 47)

Nassau Amphibious Ready Group
USS Nassau (LHA 4)
USS Austin (LPD 4)
USS Tortuga (LSD 46)

**Iwo Jima Amphibious
Ready Group**
USS Iwo Jima (LHD 7)
USS Nashville (LPD 13)
USS Carter Hall (LSD 50)

Mine Countermeasures Div 31
USS Ardent (MCM 12)
USS Dextrous (MCM 13)
USS Cardinal (MHC 60)
USS Raven (MHC 61)

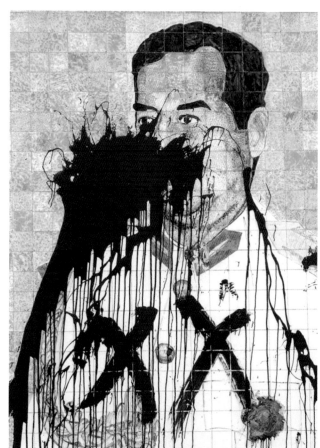